Neston & Parkgate

REMEMBERED

Jeffrey Pearson

I dedicate this book to the memory of
IAN ROBERT WILLIAMS R.N.
a Neston man who died in the Falkland War
at the age of twenty-one.

First published 1998 by Countyvise Limited, 14 Appin Road,
Birkenhead L41 9HH

Copyright © 1998 Jeffrey Pearson.

The right of Jeffrey Pearson to be identified as the author of this work has been
asserted by him in accordance with the Copyright, Design and Patents Act 1988.

British Library Cataloguing in Publication Data.
A catalogue record for this book is available from the British Library.

ISBN 1 901231 07 0

Scene at Neston Station on the G.W. & L.W.R. joint line before the First World War.
(Collection Ian Boumphrey)

Contents

𝔍llustrations

List of Maps

Introduction

I have written this book in response to the many requests I have received for a fuller version of my "Neston and Parkgate" (published Countyvise 1985)

"Neston and Parkgate Remembered" deals with the same geographical area as the earlier book, that is the area comprising the ancient townships of Great Neston, Little Neston, Ness, and Leighton. (Parkgate was a comparatively late settlement, and stands partly in the township of Great Neston and partly in Leighton). In other words, an area corresponding to the modern Anglican parish.

Although I have been obliged to repeat the essential core material contained in the first book, by writing this revised and enlarged version, I have been able to include much extra material, some of it unearthed since 1985.

For this new book I have adopted the same format as I used for "Neston and Parkgate". That is, I have presented a chronological account of the Area's history, followed by a number of appendices dealing with specific topics. Most of the chapter headings correspond to those in the earlier book, but I have not included an appendix on Ness Gardens - the former Director of Ness Gardens, Ken Hulme, has written a book on the subject. I have, however, added an appendix on the Cottage Hospital.

I have concluded this book at the same date that I concluded "Neston and Parkgate" - March 1974, when the former Neston and Ellesmere Port local authorities were merged to form the Borough of Ellesmere Port and Neston.

Jeffrey Pearson

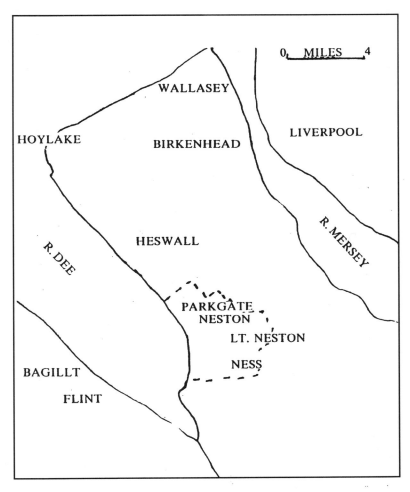

Map 1: Location Map of the Neston Area

Chapter One

The Early Years

Although the townships in the Neston Area were all, with one partial exception, basically Saxon, enough circumstantial evidence has been discovered to suggest there was some occupation of the Area as early as Roman times.

Over the course of the last hundred and fifty years, or so, a number of Roman artefacts have been unearthed, including coins, the rim shards of two jars, and a trumpet brooch, but the most convincing evidence of pre-Saxon occupation has been discovered during current excavation of the Romano-British farmhouse at Irby, in the form of slag with traces of coal which has been identified as having come from what, later, became the Neston Area. The leader of the dig, Dr. Rob Philpott, believes that the coal is likely to have been used in the farm workshops, where metal items were made and repaired.

It is a find that does not leave too much room for doubt about the existence of some settlement in the present Ness-cum-Denhall area during Roman times. Coins, brooches, and jars, could all have been accidentally dropped by travellers passing through the Neston Area over the course of two or three centuries; working the local coal seam would have necessitated the miners living close to their pits.

Just how long these Celtic miners remained in the Area, and whether their successors saw the arrival of the Saxons will, probably, never be known. What is certain is that they left nothing in the way of landmarks or place names to testify to their passing.

So, with one exception, the settlements of the Neston Area, as they have existed for a thousand years and more, were established by Saxons. Denhall's name (Danewell) indicates that its origins were Norse.

At some time during the tenth century a large number of Danes or Vikings - the terms are generally accepted as interchangeable - who had settled in Ireland, were expelled from the Dublin area. Some settled in the Isle of Man, and some came to Wirral. Those who landed on Wirral would soon have discovered that there were many well-established Saxon settlements here, but that there was also space enough for them to found their own farms and villages without conflict.

The two racial groups seem to have co-existed peacefully. There is some evidence to indicate that they traded and co-operated freely with each other and, what is certain, that, increasingly over the years, they mingled and inter-married until the ethnic distinctions between them had disappeared.

Evidence that this cultural cross-fertilisation may have begun early in the Neston Area can be seen in five carved sandstone cross fragments which were unearthed when the old Neston church was being demolished in 1874. For a century and more, they were generally regarded as Saxon, but, after he had examined them in 1986, Dr. R.H. White, of Liverpool University, pronounced them to be fragments of Irish-Viking commemorative crosses, dating from the period 930 to about 1020 AD. These stones are now displayed in the Church nave.

Neston, or Great Neston, as it was known until about eighty years ago, was always the most important settlement in the Area. The first syllable of its name, "nes", is derived from the Anglo-Saxon word for a headland, "nesse" or "naze". "Ton" is a typical Saxon ending for a settlement, which could be as small as an individual farm or as big as a village.

So Neston was "the settlement by the headland". To-day, there is no sign of a headland, but it certainly existed. Speed's map of Cheshire, dated 1611, clearly shows a promontory jutting into the Dee Estuary from a point close to the town. In addition, we have the eye-witness evidence of Daniel Defoe, best remembered as the author of "Robinson Crusoe". In 1700 Defoe came to Wirral, collecting material for his book, "A Tour Through the Whole Island of Great Britain" (published in 1724-26). In it he wrote:

> *Going down from Chester by the Rhoodee as they call it, that is the marshes of the river Dee, and coasting the river after it had grown broader than the marshes, the first place of any note we come to is Nesson, a long nase or ness of land, which running out into the sea makes a kind of a key.*

At some time during the tenth century a large number of Danes or Vikings - the terms are generally accepted as interchangeable - who had settled in Ireland, were expelled from the Dublin area. Some settled in the Isle of Man, and some came to Wirral. Those who landed on Wirral would soon have discovered that there were many well-established Saxon settlements here, but that there was also space enough for them to found their own farms and villages without conflict.

The two racial groups seem to have co-existed peacefully. There is some evidence to indicate that they traded and co-operated freely with each other and, what is certain, that, increasingly over the years, they mingled and inter-married until the ethnic distinctions between them had disappeared.

Evidence that this cultural cross-fertilisation may have begun early in the Neston Area can be seen in five carved sandstone cross fragments which were unearthed when the old Neston church was being demolished in 1874. For a century and more, they were generally regarded as Saxon, but, after he had examined them in 1986, Dr. R.H. White, of Liverpool University, pronounced them to be fragments of Irish-Viking commemorative crosses, dating from the period 930 to about 1020 AD. These stones are now displayed in the Church nave.

Neston, or Great Neston, as it was known until about eighty years ago, was always the most important settlement in the Area. The first syllable of its name, "nes", is derived from the Anglo-Saxon word for a headland, "nesse" or "naze". "Ton" is a typical Saxon ending for a settlement, which could be as small as an individual farm or as big as a village.

So Neston was "the settlement by the headland". To-day, there is no sign of a headland, but it certainly existed. Speed's map of Cheshire, dated 1611, clearly shows a promontory jutting into the Dee Estuary from a point close to the town. In addition, we have the eye-witness evidence of Daniel Defoe, best remembered as the author of "Robinson Crusoe". In 1700 Defoe came to Wirral, collecting material for his book, "A Tour Through the Whole Island of Great Britain" (published in 1724-26). In it he wrote:

> Going down from Chester by the Rhoodee as they call it, that is the marshes of the river Dee, and coasting the river after it had grown broader than the marshes, the first place of any note we come to is Nesson, a long nase or ness of land, which running out into the sea makes a kind of a key.

Unfortunately for the Abbey, Ralph's action was resented by his nephew Roger de Montalt, Chief Justice of Chester and, in his own time, Lord of the Manor of Neston. An entry in the Chronicle, dated 1258, records that Roger entered the Church with a body of armed men, and turned out the monks who had been sent from the Abbey to perform the services. He then gave the living to his own nephew, Ralph.

When, however, the Abbot offered him a manor in return for the living, Roger promptly retrieved the living from his nephew, and closed the bargain.

The Abbey authorities were nothing if not vindictive. The chronicler concludes his account of the affair by listing the misfortunes that befell Roger, as a warning to other would-be robbers of the Church. He recorded that Roger's eldest son died within fifteen days, and that Roger himself,

> ....*died in poverty within two years, the common people being ignorant of the place of his burial.*

The living of Neston Church remained in the hands of the Abbots of Chester until the Dissolution of the Abbey in 1540, when it passed into the authority of the Dean and Chapter of Chester Cathedral.

It was Roger de Montalt who established Neston Park (See Map 2). A deer park of some two hundred acres, it was a feature of the town from about 1250 until the middle of the seventeenth century, and its existence is still recalled in the names of Park Street, Parks Field, and, Parkgate.

Chester Customs Accounts reveal that Neston and Denhall, like a number of other settlements along the Dee coast, were used as anchorages during the Middle Ages.

In the earliest years this seems to have been because the vessels concerned were too heavily laden to reach Chester. In later years, however, increasing use of the estuary anchorages was forced on ships' masters by the silting which, increasingly, obstructed the approaches to Chester. The basic cause of the silting problem was the poor scour of the river. Dee tides flow rapidly, but ebb slowly. The fast-moving flood carries with it a heavy load of silt, which is allowed to settle on the bed of the estuary by the sluggish ebb. Over the centuries the layers of mud spread by successive tides rose to the point where they denied the City's wharves to all but shallow-draught river craft.

The Custom Records, which survive from 1301 onwards, provide details of the ships which arrived at the City and at its estuary anchorages. They

*The Old Parish Church c1870, from a painting by Harold Hopps
(Collection Williamson Art Gallery). This Church, much altered and
extended over the centuries, stood on the same site as present Parish
Church from, at least, 1180, until it was demolished in 1875.*

reveal that, of the nine estuary anchorages mentioned[*], Denhall was one
of the most frequently-used, while only the occasional ship unloaded at
Neston Park - later to develop as Parkgate.

They also reveal that the bulk of Chester's seaborne trade was with the
Irish ports of Dublin, Waterford, and Wexford. Prominent among the Irish-
bound cargoes were salt, coal (presumably from North Wales), and items
described as "small wares" e.g. wooden cups, hemp ropes, and saffron.
Goods shipped in from Ireland included hides and other animal skins -
sheep, badger, and rabbit - rolls of checked cloth, tallow, and butts of
sack.

---

[*] *West Kirby, Redbank (Dawpool), Heswall, Gayton, Neston Park, Denhall, Burton,
Shotwick, Portpool. (Location of Portpool not now known, but described by the
sixteenth century writer Leland as being "a couple of bow shots of the suburbs
outside the Northgate.")*

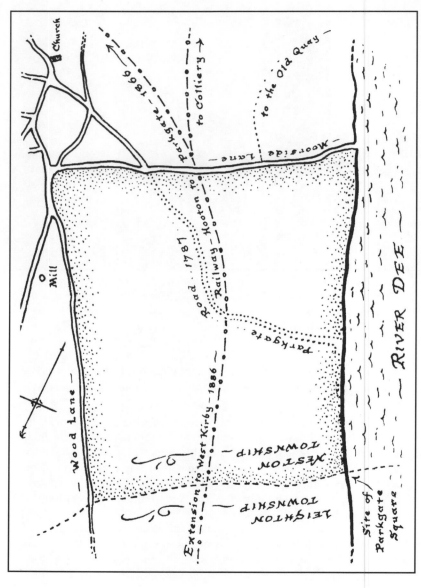

Map 2. Sketch map to show the location of Neston (deer) Park, using modern road names to mark the boundaries.

While the Irish traffic represented the Port's bread and butter trade, ships arrived at the Dee from many parts of Western Europe, and a particularly brisk trade developed between Chester and various ports in France and Spain.

Imports from France seem to have been almost exclusively of wine, but those from Spain were much more varied. While wine and iron were both prominent, other frequent imports included: olive oil; spices; honey; figs; tar; wax; and liquorice.

A particularly vivid illustration of the rich variety of the Spanish trade is afforded an entry in the Records which notes that, in June 1526, "The St. Mary of Caminha" arrived at Denhall from Spain with: 38 pipes of wine (4,788 gallons); 3 hogsheads of oil (189 gallons); 30 pounds of wax; 20 kintails (2,000 lbs.) of cork; 3 pounds of cloves; 24 cordovan skins; 3 coffers of sugar; and 1 kintel of raisins.

More typical were "The Katherine of St. Malo", which anchored off Neston Park with 15 tons of Spanish iron in May 1476, and "The St. Michael of Legueitio", which arrived at Denhall with 50 tuns of Spanish wine in May 1495.

Regular outward cargoes to the Continent included salt, calves' skins, both tanned and untanned, a type of woollen cloth known, for some obscure reason, as "Manchester Cotton", and tallow.

These goods were transported between the ships and Chester by river craft. In those days of atrocious roads it was the only practicable way to move such bulk cargoes.

While the arrival of a ship must always have been an event for the locals, the sight of a fleet of some sixty vessels anchoring off Neston in the autumn of 1282 must have caused a sensation. Despatched from the Cinque ports to assist King Edward I to crush a Welsh uprising led by David ap Gruffydd, the fleet lay off the village for several days while the troops, who arrived by boat from Chester, embarked and then set sail for Anglesey. The attack was launched the following spring, and ap Gruffydd was defeated after a six-month campaign.

To these isolated glimpses of medieval Neston may be added the inference that it was an essentially agricultural settlement, and that it was a place of some local importance.

That Neston was an agricultural settlement may be deduced from the earliest surviving map, drawn for the Mostyn estate in 1732, which bears clear evidence of an extensive medieval open field system.

That it was a place of local importance may be inferred from the fact that it was the centre of a parish which included no fewer than eight townships: Great and Little Neston, Ness-cum-Denhall, Raby, Leighton, Ledsham, Thornton Hough, and Willaston. It was to Neston that the inhabitants of this extensive area were obliged to come for baptisms, weddings, funerals and any other business demanded by the Church's customs and Calendar, and it was to Neston that the officials of the Abbey would have to come when their duties obliged them to visit their parishes

Little more is known about medieval Neston. It is a place almost covered by the mists of historical obscurity: something can be seen, but the bulk lies hidden.

SOURCES NOT MENTIONED IN THE TEXT

"Chartulary of Chester Abbey 533" (Chetham Society Vol 82) Recognizance Roll 234, in "Cheshire Sheaf" April 1923

Dodgson, J. McN. "The Place Names of Cheshire" (Cambridge 1969-70)

Hewitt, H. J. "Cheshire Under the Three Edwards" (Cheshire Community Council, 1967)

Leland, John "The Itinerary in Wales of John Leland" (c 1536-39, ed. L Toulmin-Smith, vol. 3 of 5, 1907-10)

Mostyn Papers (Bangor, 5850)

Plea Rolls, Chester 29/35

University of London Institute for Historical Research "The Victoria History of the County of Chester" (Oxford) 1987

Wakefield, Helen "Revealing Secrets of Roman Remains" (Article in Wirral News, 20th July 1994)

Wilson, K .P. "Chester Customs Accounts 1301-1565" (Record Society of Lancashire and Cheshire) 1969

White, R. H. "Viking-Period Sculpture at Neston, Cheshire" (Journal of the Chester Archaeological Society, Volume 69. 1986)

Chapter Two

The New Quay

The mists of historical obscurity finally cleared from Neston in the mid-sixteenth century, when a quay to handle Chester's shipping trade was built close to the village.

Many of the details concerned with the construction and business of the "New Quay" or "New Haven", as it was known, were recorded in various surviving documents, which, together, convey an impression of Elizabethan/Jacobean Neston as a bustling, prosperous, and rapidly-expanding town.

The construction of the Quay represented an attempt by Chester Town Assembly to protect the City's seaborne trade, which was threatened by the continuing silting of the Estuary. The layers of silt spread by successive tides increasingly blocked the approaches to Chester until, in 1541, the City Assembly, convinced it was facing a crisis, petitioned the King's Council to grant them help to build a new quay at Neston.

The site selected was about half a mile to the south-west of Neston, at a place called "Lightfoot's Poole". The reasons for this choice appear to have been the shelter offered by the naze, or promontory, that existed there, and the deep water that was found inshore at that point. Although no contemporary survey records now exist, when the royal hydrographer, Captain Greenville Collins, conducted a survey of the Dee between 1684 and 1689 i.e. some 150 years later when the river was presumably shallower, he recorded the depth of water thereabouts as being between thirty and forty feet at spring tides. (See Map 3)

Work began about 1545.

At first the stones were hewed from a quarry near Chester, and brought down river by barge, but from February 1568 they were obtained from a new quarry at Little Neston.

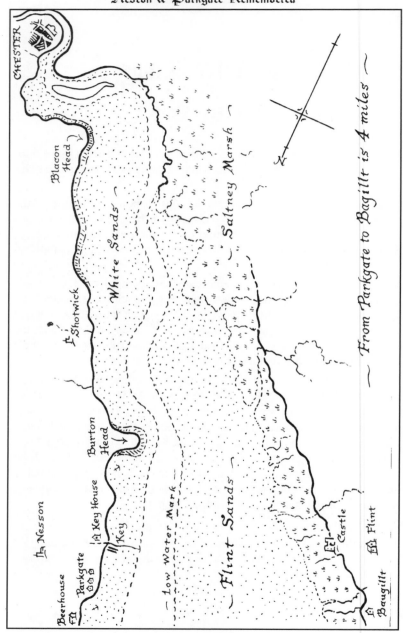

Map 3. The Dee Estuary in 1684. Adapted from Captain Greenville Collins's chart.

An examination of Thomas Boydell's map of 1771 (See Map 5) shows the Quay jutting directly out into the river from the point of what appears to be the artificially-straightened naze.

Incredibly, the planners and engineers do not seem to have realised that to construct a massive stone pier out into the Estuary at a point where the tides flowed at their strongest, and which was completely exposed to the winter gales, would be a difficult, slow, and money-consuming business.

The records of the work at Chester Record Office are now incomplete, but, from the those which remain, it is clear that progress was hindered by frequent storm damage. So much so that the Assembly never managed to keep the pier in good repair for long.

The original costings seem to have been completely inadequate because, in 1557 and, again, in 1560, the Assembly was obliged to seek more help from central government, which, on both occasions, responded by ordering special collections towards the cost of the quay to be made in churches throughout the country. Even so, the work dragged on until 1604, when the Assembly refused to invest any more capital in it. It seems probable that the original plans were never completely realised.

No pictorial representation of the pier survives, but it seems that it comprised parallel facings of great stones, and, between them, fillings of small or great stones. The north, or down estuary, side, was fitted with embrasures for cannons. The only indication we have to its size occurs in an entry in the Assembly's records made in 1598, when the Haven wall was, not for the first time, in danger of collapsing:

> *The decay of the New Haven to witt 56 footes in length, in bredth or thickness 24 footes and in height, beside the battlements, 12 is decayed and fallen down..........*

Despite the problems involved in its construction, large quantities of merchandise and a considerable number of passengers passed over the Quay, while it was still being built, and throughout the seventeenth century.

Writing in 1615, William Webb referred to Neston in the following terms:

> *The well-known town parish, church and port of Great Neston, and the usual place where our passengers into Ireland do so often lie waiting the leisure of the winds, which make many people better acquainted with this place than they desire to be, though there be wanting no convenient entertainment, if no other lie in the way;*

11

and here is station of the ships called 'The New Key", where they embark and disembark both men, horses, kine and all other commodities on the back of this Neston.

(King's Vale Royal)

Although it was another century before the incumbents of Neston started to record the occupations of those whose names they entered on the Parish Registers, it seems reasonable to deduce from Webb's comments that in his time the town was thriving by providing accommodation and services for the passengers who were waiting to embark for Ireland, and from handling the cargoes which passed over the Quay.

Many of the passengers and much of the freight moved between Chester and the Quay in small vessels. An observer writing in 1620 noted:

West Chester: There is a piece of ground a mile about encompassed with water called the Roe Dee, where barks of some 20 or 30 tons come up from Nesson, which carry passengers into and out of Ireland.

Those passengers who chose the overland route between the two places, by coach, on foot, or by some other means, followed the road which, from Neston, passed over Neston Bridge, through the townships of Little Neston, Ness, and Burton, and then on to Shotwick, either by a track through Puddington, or by a path which went down to the edge of the river and came out just below Shotwick Church, traces of which can still be seen. After crossing the creek at Shotwick, the traveller could either follow the old military road through the park and King's Wood, or take a shorter, but somewhat more hazardous route, along the sands.

Dee ships seldom exceeded 100 tons displacement, and few Neston-registered ships displaced more than 80 tons.

The names of many of the local ships and ship owners are recorded in Chester City archives. For example, in 1571 licences to sail from the Port of Chester (which included the New Quay) to certain other specified ports were granted on the 23rd and 25th May by the Mayor, Sir Lawrence Smith, to the following vessels:

Richard Bennett, of Neston, and Wm. Waley, of the same: 'The Trinitie' of Neston, which belongeth to the aforesaid Richard.

William Waley, of Neston, and Richard Bennett, of the same: 'The Marten' of Neston, which belongeth to the aforesaid William.

Roger Garrett, of Neston, and John Lawsley, of the same: 'The Katherine of Neston,' which belongeth to the aforesaid John.

12

In addition to the well-established Irish and western European trade, new commercial links were forged with the Baltic states, which supplied such commodities as timber, pitch, and fish, in return for coal, salt, and manufactured goods.

The Quay was often used by troops on their journeys between England and Ireland. Particularly noteworthy, perhaps, were the 2,000 soldiers who landed there, from Ireland, on the 6th December 1643, to reinforce Chester's Royalist garrison during the Civil War, and a further 1,300 reinforcements who disembarked there on 7th February 1644.

Gradually, silting made access to the Quay increasingly difficult, and ships began to anchor a mile, or so, further downstream, opposite the site of the former Neston (deer) Park. The Quay seems to have fallen into disuse by the early 1700s, and it had certainly done so by 1732, when John Mackay marked it on his map of the estuary as 'The Old Quay', a name that was adopted by all subsequent cartographers.

In 1759 the pier was described as being "In ruinous condition", and in 1799 Chester Assembly sold the dressed stones to Sir Roger Mostyn, Lord of the Manor of Neston. According to local tradition, many of the stone blocks were used to build the present sea wall at Parkgate.

Until 1943 a building known as "The Old Quay House" stood as the last substantial relic of the Haven (Illustration 3). Almost certainly built as a custom house - a customs officer was recorded at Neston in the early 1600s - in the course of its three hundred-and-fifty year history, it also served a number of other roles, including that of an inn, in the late seventeenth and early eighteenth centuries; a House of Correction for unemployed Irish labourers who were being forcibly returned to their own parishes, in the second half of the eighteenth century; and, at various times, a private dwelling. Unoccupied for the last forty years of its existence, gaunt and eerie in its isolation by the marshes, the building was a magnet to the local children, who were attracted by the spine-chilling stories of ghosts that had gathered around it. Gradually, the structure deteriorated to the point where it was judged to be dangerous, and reduced to the safe heap of rubble that may still be seen today with Home Guard hand-grenades.

In the meantime, two miles inland from the bustle of the Quay, Neston's first recorded school was established on Windle Hill in 1610.

Nothing now remains to indicate the exact site, but, from documentary references, it seems probable that it stood on the corner of what is now known as Quarry Road and School Lane.

3. The Old Quay House, photographed c1930.

14

As a church school, it was subject to inspection by the Diocesan Authorities, and a report on such a 'visitation' made by Bishop Francis Gastrell in 1717, noted

Here is a School in this township which is near the center of the whole (old) parish, about a mile from Neston, which is repaired by the Parish, but when and by whom built is not known......................Master is nominated by the Vicar of Neston and the Churchwardens. School 10 yards long and 5 yards broad.

This school remained in use for some 150 years.

SOURCES NOT MENTIONED IN THE TEXT

Cheshire Record Office DHL 3/9, 11

Gastrell, Francis "Notitia Cestriensis, 1717, Vol.1" (Chetham Society, 1845)

Morris, R. H. "Chester in the Plantagenet and Stuart Reigns" (Chester, 1894)

Place, G. "The Rise and Fall of Parkgate, Passenger Port for Ireland 1686-1815" (The Chetham Society, 1994)

Ridout, Edna "The Chester Companies and The Old Quay." (Transactions of The Historic Society of Lancashire and Cheshire.1927)

Symonds, Richard "Diary of the Marches of the Royal Army During the Civil War". ed. C.E. Long (Camden Society, 1859)

Wilson, K. P. "Chester Customs Accounts 1301 - 1565" (Record Society of Lancashire and Cheshire, 1969)

Woodward, D. M. "The Trade of Elizabethan Chester" (Hull, 1970)

Young, Peter "The English Civil War Armies" (Reading, 1973)

Chapter Three

The Boom

As silting rendered the approaches to Neston Quay increasingly more difficult, ships' masters increasingly anchored their vessels further downstream at Parkgate, until, by the early eighteenth century, the Quay had become almost inaccessible, and Parkgate had become Chester's main outport.

In passing, it should be noted that not all masters chose to use Neston Quay or Parkgate in the seventeenth century, and that a third Neston anchorage was still in use, at Denhall, until the tail end of the century.

In the early seventeenth century, "Parkgate" seems to have been little more than the name of an anchorage. It possessed no facilities for the handling of passengers or cargoes, and there is no record of any buildings there.

It was, however, still well within the Parish of Neston, and close enough to the town for ship owners to benefit from the amenities which had developed there for the convenience of passengers, and from some of the facilities still available there for the handling of the sort of cargoes which had passed over Neston Quay. Among the diverse service occupations recorded in the eighteenth century Parish Registers were those of carriers, carpenters, wheelwrights, blacksmiths, inn-keepers, tailors, shoemakers, barbers, chaisemen, apothecaries, chirurgeons (doctors), an attorney-at-law, and at least one pawnbroker.

The seventeenth and eighteenth centuries were nothing less than a boom time for the Neston Area.

A petition of 1728 addressed by the Lord of the Manor, Sir Roger Mostyn, to the King, requesting permission for the establishment of a market at Great Neston stated:

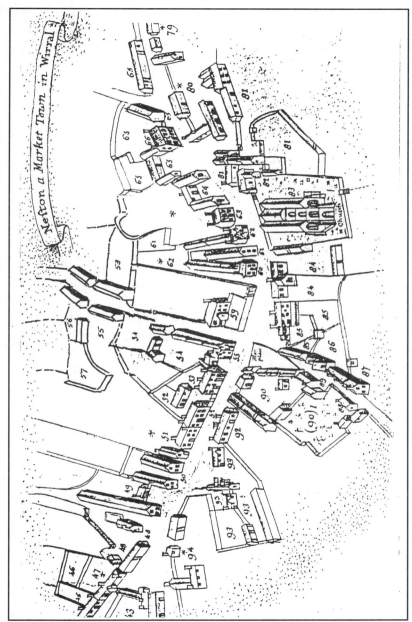

Map 4. An Extract from the Mostyn Estate Map of 1732, depicting the centre of Great Neston.
Note the location of the Market Place on the Cross. Some of the buildings marked, such as the Brewers' Arms
and its sandstone barn, are still standing.

.....Great Neston is not only the largest and best town in this (Wirral) Hundred, but very much the most conveniently situated for a market, being very near the middle of the Hundred, and in the midway between Chester and Hoylake, and is itself a port for all or most of the ships of any bulk that have any trade with the City or County of Chester, (and) is a place where most officers of the Army or people of quality take shipping for Ireland and land on their return from that Kingdom.

The petition was successful. The right to hold a weekly market on Fridays, and a fair three times a year, was conferred on Sir Roger and his heirs by a royal charter, granted on 25th September 1728.

It was a development which confirmed the status of Great Neston as a town, and brought an additional prosperity to the Area with the buyers and sellers who were drawn to the markets and fairs from all parts of Cheshire and North Wales.

At first, Parkgate's trade followed much the same pattern as that which had passed over Neston Quay. Chester Port books show that the most important exports were coal and salt to Ireland, and lead to continental countries. The lead originated in the North Wales mines, and was transported from Bagillt to Parkgate in lighters. There it was transhipped to the sea-going vessels, which were too large to use the Bagillt anchorage.

Imports included linen and animal products, such as tallow, skins, and hides, from Ireland, timber, tar, and flax from the Baltic states, and wine and cork from Portugal.

In 1732 the costs of transporting goods between Parkgate and Chester were quoted as 2 shillings a ton by boat, and 6 shillings per ton overland. Considerable in the terms of the time.

In an attempt to reduce these costs, the stretch of river between Chester and Golfyn, on the Welsh side, was canalised between 1733 and 1737. This "New Cut" was eighty feet wide, and gave a depth of fifteen feet at spring tides. Enough width and depth to allow sea-going ships to moor at the City's wharves. It also had the effect of forcing the first eight miles of the main channel below Chester away from its natural course, on the Wirral side of the Estuary, to the Welsh side, and made possible the reclamation of that stretch of the old river bed now known as "Sealand".

As soon as it escaped from the grasp of the Cut, at Golftyn, however, the water turned north, and made its way across the Estuary to Parkgate, from where it resumed its old course. It was a situation that persisted for some seventy to eighty years (See Map 5). Until, that is, the embankment on the north side of the cut was extended far enough to train the channel completely over to the Welsh side.

While much effort and capital investment was sunk into The New Cut, it did not have the desired effect of eliminating the need to tranship goods at Parkgate. The contemporary "Register of shipping entering or leaving the port of Chester", reveals that the transfer of goods from one form of transport to another at Parkgate was still common in the second half of the eighteenth century.

That second half of the century saw developments of trade in two cargoes, which were to become important for the Neston Area itself, rather than for the parent port of Chester.

The first was a revival of an old traffic. For the greater part of the seventeenth century large numbers of cattle had been unloaded at Neston Quay and Parkgate, but this traffic had been brought to an end by the Irish Cattle Act of 1681, an Act designed to protect the English fatstock market. In 1759 the Act was repealed, and the following years saw a steady increase in landings of cows, sheep, and pigs at Parkgate.

Local tradition holds that, before the sea wall was built, the animals were landed opposite the site now occupied by "Alma Cottage", and penned there until they were driven away to their final destination. After work started on the wall, about 1800, they were landed at the slipway which may still be seen in the length of sea wall between the north end of Parkgate and Gayton Cottage, and penned in the field immediately behind it.

By the early nineteenth century the Area's livestock trade was, again, considerable. For example, "The Chester Courant" of 22nd January 1811 reported that, during the second six months of 1810, 2,580 cows, 3,386 pigs, 1,762 sheep, and 160 horses had been landed at Parkgate from Ireland.

The second trade which developed in the second half of the eighteenth century was in the export of local coal. In the early 1760s a mine was opened on the coast at Ness, and a stone quay was built to handle the coal. According to an advertisement which appeared in "The Courant" of 29th August 1812, it was exported to Ireland, North and South Wales, and The Isle of Man. (See Appendix B)

It was, however, primarily as a passenger port that Parkgate flourished during the eighteenth century.

Among the passengers who used the port were many distinguished figures, including Jonathan Swift, Dean of St. Patrick's Cathedral, Dublin, and author of "Gulliver's Travels," who passed through Parkgate on a number of occasions between 1704 and 1713; George Frederick Handel, who disembarked there in 1742, on his return from Dublin, where he had conducted the first performance of "Messiah"; and the great itinerant preacher John Wesley.

Wesley passed through Parkgate on nine occasions on his preaching journeys to and from Ireland, and made a number of, mainly cursory, references to the port in his Journal. One, slightly longer, entry describes an incident that occurred in 1762:

> *Friday April 1st. I rode to Parkgate and found several ships, but the wind was contrary. I preached at five in the small house they have just built, and the hearers were remarkably serious. I gave notice of preaching in the morning. But half an hour after four, one brought us word that Captain Jordan would sail in less than an hour. We were soon in the ship, wherein we found about threescore passengers.*

A Methodist congregation had been established at Neston in the 1750s, and the new "small house" to which the entry refers was a chapel that stood a little back from Parkgate Road (illustration 6). There was much general hostility to Methodists at the time, and the Chapel was deliberately located in a secluded position to make observation of worshippers more difficult. The building no longer exists, but a roadside plaque marks the spot.

Before 1785 the vast majority of passengers travelling between Parkgate and Ireland did so on what were primarily cargo vessels. Travellers were only able to secure passage when they found a loaded cargo ship bound for their port of destination. When John Wesley crossed from Parkgate in 1762 he was obliged to climb over a stack of bagged hops to get into his cabin.

The exceptional few were those privileged to travel on the Royal Yacht. From the early 1660s until the early 1830s the Royal Navy placed a succession of yachts at the disposal of the Lord Lieutenants of Ireland. These yachts were used to carry distinguished passengers -usually members of the nobility or gentry - between Parkgate and Dublin. They were also used to transport money to pay the Army stationed in Ireland. They were the only Royal Navy vessels to visit Parkgate regularly, and they are commemorated in the name of "The Yacht Inn" at Woodbank, on the Chester High Road.

The situation changed in 1785, when the Parkgate Packet Company was formed, for the purpose of providing a regular passenger service between Parkgate and Dublin. The venture was launched with a single vessel "The King", of 100 tons, which was joined in the following year by a second "The Queen", also of 100 tons. Both were Parkgate built. By 1792 the Company's fleet had expanded to six.

The opening of a turnpike road between Chester and Parkgate in 1787 represented a further development to benefit travellers. The Chester High Road (Now the A540) was, in fact, already in existence as an ancient highway that gave access to Parkgate by way of Neston Cross and Moorside Lane. In 1787, the road was widened, and a final half mile stretch built across land previously occupied by Neston Park to Parkgate. (See Map 2). Other roads connected Neston and Parkgate to the villages of Birkenhead and Tranmere, and to the Mersey ferries. These roads, together with the Irish Packet Service and the ferry services that connected Parkgate with Bagillt and Flint, on the Welsh coast, established Neston as the main communications centre on the Peninsula. It was a period when contemporary gazeteers indicated the position of all other towns and villages on Wirral by describing them as being;

.......*situated at...........miles from Great Neston*

From about the middle of the century, when sea bathing became fashionable, both for pleasure and for the supposed medicinal properties of seawater, Parkgate gradually assumed an additional role: that of a holiday resort. Indeed, it became one of the best-known bathing places in the country.

Of course, in the eighteenth and early nineteenth centuries only the wealthy and their dependants could afford holidays. The idea of holidays for working folk would have been inconceivable.

In 1785 Parkgate was visited by Emma Lyon, later to become Lady Hamilton, and mistress of Lord Nelson. Born a blacksmith's daughter at Ness, some twenty-one years previously, she returned from London, where she was living as the mistress of the Honourable Charles Greville M.P., to treat a skin complaint by bathing in seawater. Together with her mother and infant daughter, she stayed at the house of a Mrs. Darnwood, said to be Dover Cottage, the last house in Station Road nearest the sea front. During her stay, Emma used the name 'Mrs. Hart', presumably as a cloak of respectability to cover her shame as the mother of an illegitimate child.

21

Writing to Greville from Parkgate Emma reported;

> *The sea-watter has done me much good. I have drunk a tumbler*
> *glas every morning fasting, walked half-an-hour, and then bathed*
> *and breakfasted. I am oblidged to a give a shilling a day for the*
> *bathing horse and whoman, and twopence a day for the dress. It is*
> *a great expense, and it frets me wen I think of it.*

Other notable visitors to the resort, included Mrs. Maria Fitzherbert, the first wife of the Prince of Wales - later King George IV, and the great painter J. M. W. Turner.

Mrs Fitzherbert is said to have stayed at the Talbot Inn - now a private house, "Green Shutters" - in 1798 or 1799. On one occasion she heard that about 700 soldiers were camped nearby, waiting for the ships that were to take them to Ireland. Told that their food was poor, she paid for them to receive an additional daily ration of a quarter of sheep, and a measure of potatoes (whatever that might have been) for every seven men.

The fact that Turner visited Parkgate was established by the late Norman Ellison, a local naturalist and writer, who discovered an engraving from a Turner dated 1794 in an old volume of "The Copper Plate Magazine and Itinerant." Entitled "Flint from Parkgate," it depicts a farm with a field of stooked corn, and two figures with dogs in the Wirral foreground, several ships in sail on the Dee, and Flint Castle and the Welsh Hills in the background.

Richard Ayton, in a book which described a journey he made round the country in the summer of 1813, "A Voyage Round Great Britain", recorded his impressions of Parkgate when he arrived there from by ferry boat from Wales in the following terms;

> *The little town of Parkgate, whose single row of houses, gaily*
> *decorated in whitewash and red ochre, may be seen and admired*
> *from afar. We landed again in our native land at this place, and in*
> *our walk from the boat to the inn had an opportunity of seeing all*
> *that it holds out to the curiosity and amusement of a stranger. It*
> *was built solely for bathers, but has the misfortune to be in the*
> *worst situation that could be desired for their accommodation. We*
> *are generally content in these kinds of establishments to give up all*
> *other conveniences for the sake of salt water, but here that is given*
> *up for two-thirds of a day, and in exchange for it one has the*
> *satisfaction of seeing from every window of his house a dismal waste*
> *of sand, and that too so soft and so intersected by deep*

22

furrows that it is not passable with comfort by man or horse. One may reckon, indeed, with certainty on a dip every day, but it is exceedingly annoying to be remodelling your engagements and inclinations according to the irregularity of the tide's attendance. The condition of visitors at low water is truly deplorable, but, having lingered through the full penance of the ebb tide, their spirits rise with the flood, and at high water there is general burst of business and animation. We arrived at just such a juncture, when the beach was all alive, and discovered a spectacle which a foreigner might have moralised upon with more seriousness than we of this free country can be permitted to do. Few of either sex thought it necessary to hide themselves under the awnings of bathing machines: posts with ropes fastened to them are fixed in the sands, and these were taken possession of by numerous groups of women, six or seven in a row, shouting, laughing, and screaming, evidently as careless of being seen as being drowned.

The most enduring of the amenities provided for the fashionable visitors who came to Parkgate is the sea wall, which was built as a promenade wall. It was never a quay. Although Parkgate was an anchorage throughout the eighteenth century no quay or jetty was constructed to facilitate the handling of traffic during that period. Ships anchored in the main channel, some hundred yards or so from the village, and passengers and goods were rowed ashore.

The first part of the wall to be built was the middle section, from the Watch House to the bulge in the wall which to-day encloses that part of the Parade known as "The Donkey Stand". The wall bulged at that point to skirt a tall narrow building that stood there. Built originally as a custom house, it became Parkgate's first Assembly House about 1780. This first section of the wall was built between 1800 and 1810, reputedly with stones reclaimed from the Old Neston Quay.

The Assembly House was the social centre of the resort, where visitors met to dance, play cards, and otherwise socialise. After the first Assembly House had been converted into seawater baths in 1812, a new one was opened in the building now known as Balcony House.

Among the other places of entertainment offered by the Area were an occasional theatre, a billiard room, several coffee shops, and two racecourses (See Illustration 4)

GREAT NESTON RACES.

N *Whit-Monday*, the 27th of *May*, 1765, will be run for, A PURSE of FIFTY POUNDS. Four Years old Horses, &c. to carry Eight Stone, and all others to carry Weight for Age.—Subject to Articles.

On *Tuesday*, the 28th, A PURSE of FIFTY POUNDS, Fourteen Hands to carry Nine Stone; all under or over to carry Weight for Inches.——Subject to Articles.

Every Horse, &c. to be shewn and entered at the *Golden Lion*, in GREAT NESTON, on *Friday* before the Days of Running, between Two and Six in the Afternoon; and such Horses, &c. to be kept in the Town 'till the Days of Running, at such Houses as subscribe Five Shillings. An Ordinary at the *Golden Lion* each Race Day, a Cocking each Morning, and a BALL for the Ladies as usual.

All Persons who live out of the Parish of GREAT NESTON that intend to have a Booth to sell any Liquor on the Course, are to pay Five Shillings into the Hands of the Clerks of the Course on the Days of entering the Horses; and such Persons who live in the Parish that have a Booth, are to pay on that Day 2s. 6d. into the Hands of the Clerks.

N. B. If any Person erects Booths, &c. contrary to the above, will be prosecuted by the Lord of the Manor.

CHESTER: Printed by READ and HUXLEY, over the *Eastgate*.

4. *(opposite) Neston Races, which were first run in 1728, continued as an annual Whitsuntide event until about 1850. The original racecourse, and the one in use at the time of this poster, was located on Windle Hill. It seems however, that for some years in the early nineteeth century the Races were held at Parkgate, on a course located on Parks Field (which in those days included the land now occupied by the Springcroft Estate and the strip of country park that runs between the Estate and the present Parks Field), before they returned to the Windle Hill course at some time in the middle of the Century. The 1847 Tithe Map shows the Windle Hill course just inside the township boundary with Raby. It may be, however, that the races had already been discontinued before the Map was printed, because the last advertisements found for Neston races to date appeared in 1846. The Wirral Hunt Club revived the races, as steeplechases, on Parks Field in 1881, and meetings were held annually until 1895.*

The Golden Lion mentioned in the poster, was demolished in the 1930s. The block of shops which includes Sayers bakery now occupies the site. The "Ordinary" advertised on the poster was a set meal at a set price.

5. (left) A coin dated 1694 discovered in a wall of Sawyer's Cottage during alterations carried out in 1960 seems to indicate that this is one of the oldest buildings in Parkgate. The cottage was a public house - The Sawyer's Arms - until 1905, taking its name from its first landlord, Richard   Bartley,   who combined his duties as Mine Host with that of a carpenter. (Courtesy Jim Pratt)

6. The arrow indicates the Methodist chapel, off Parkgate Road, wher John Wesley preached in 1762. This building was demolished in the early years of this century; but a plaque marks the spot.

THEATRE PARKGATE.

On *FRIDAY Evening*, *August 9, 1811*,

Will be presented a Comedy, called

The School for Scandal.

Sir Peter Teazle	Mr. RYLEY
Sir Oliver Surface	Mr. ROSCOE
Joseph Surface	Mr. BAILIOL
Charles	Mr. WALSH
Crabtree	Mr. EDWARDS
Sir Benjamin Backbite	Mr. HOPE
Rowley	Mr. SMITH
Moses and Snake	Mr. EATON
Lady Teazle	Mrs. EDWARDS
Maria	Miss WARREN
Lady Sneerwell	Miss MONTFORD
Kitty	Mrs. BAILIOL
Mrs. Candor	Miss WALSH

END OF THE PLAY.

A COMIC SONG,   Mr. SMITH

A favorite SONG,   Mr. ROSCOE

To which will be added the laughable Farce, of

The Lying Valet.

Sharp (the Lying Valet)	Mr. EDWARDS
Justice Guttle	Mr. ROSCOE
Drunken Cook	Mr. HOPE
Beau Tripet	Mr. EATON
Gayless	Mr. SMITH
Melissa	Miss MONTFORD
Mrs. Tripet	Mrs. BAILIOL
Mrs. Gadabout	Mrs. WALSH
Kitty Pry	Miss WALSH

PIT 2s.——GALLERY 1s.

Door to be opened at six o'Clock, and to begin precisely at seven.

Tickets to be had of Mr. EDWARDS, at Mr. T. BROWN's Drury Lane, at Mr. J. DAVIES, Grocer; and at Mrs. Hall, Milliner.

CARNES, PRINTER, HOLYWELL.

7. During Parkgate's heyday as a resort, occasional theatrical performances were presented at a theatre which, according to a writer of 1879, "was situated in the lane above 'The Union'" (now reverted to its original name of 'The Ship Hotel.')

27

8. It is very possible that this building was originally a herring house and, later, the Parkgate Theatre. In correspondence with the author, Dr. A.R. Brand, of the University of Liverpool Marine Laboratory, having consulted a number of experts engaged in the herring fishing and curing industries, ventured the opinion that it had either been built as a net store or a herring house. There is, however, a clue which favours the herring house theory, in the fact that the 1879 writer, already quoted in connection with the playbill, added to his statement that the Parkgate Theatre was located in the lane behind the Union (Ship) - the site of this building - the information that it was established in a former herring house.

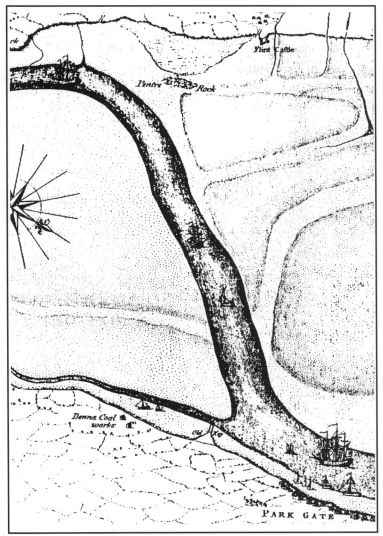

*Map 5. Map to show the changed course of the main Dee channel
following the construction of the New Cut.
Note, too, the location of Denhall Colliery and the Old (Neston) Quay.
Extract from Thomas Boydell's Map of 1771.
(Scale: Flint to Parkgate 4 miles)*

The south end of the sea wall from the Donkey Stand to the South Slipway was built about 1830, and the section from the Watch House to the North Slipway was built in the 1840s.

In addition to the activities already mentioned - those associated with a port and communications centre, a fashionable resort, a market town, and a mining area - one other contributed to the general prosperity of the Neston area, fishing. Together with its other functions, during the eighteenth and early years of the nineteenth century Parkgate was a flourishing herring curing centre. The fish were either salted or smoked in a herring house (See Illustration 8)

It is now difficult to determine whether some or all of the fish were caught by local fishermen. The fact that very few fishermen are mentioned in Neston Parish Registers for the eighteenth century may not be particularly significant. The herring season was a short one - from the end of May, or thereabouts, to the beginning of October, or thereabouts - and, according to W. C. Smith's "A Short History of the Irish Sea Herring Fisheries During the Eighteenth and Nineteenth Centuries" (Hodder & Stroughton, 1923), for the other eight months of the year the fishermen followed some other occupation, such as labourer, farmer, or mechanic. That being the case, it seems probable that the Parish Clerks recorded the occupation which a man pursued for the majority of his working time i.e. the non-fishing occupation. Equally, however, some or all of the herrings could well have been brought to Parkgate in the vessels which, Smith records, ferried the herrings, lightly salted, from the fishing boats - for the most part Manx and Irish - to the various ports where they were cured and packed in barrels. In the close season these boats were employed in the coasting trade. Any Neston Area man employed on the carrying/coasting trade would have been recorded in the Registers, with the many others who earned their livelihoods at sea, as "mariner".

As if the Neston Area did not offer enough opportunities for honest employment, smuggling appears to have been rife. During the eighteenth century customs duties were generally high, and handsome profits could be made by dealing in contraband goods.

Many custom officers were energetic in their efforts to counter this illicit trade, but in one case at least they did not have to exert themselves. According to Mrs Hilda Gamlin, on one occasion a gale smashed the rudder of a smugglers' lugger, and deposited the vessel, complete with crew and illicit cargo of salt, on the foreshore immediately under the windows of the Custom House.

In addition to the large scale-operations involving gangs, much relatively small-scale smuggling seems to have taken place. Chester Quarter Session Records for 1559-1760, includes an account of a preliminary magistrate's hearing of a case in which one Charles Lucas, a seaman, was charged with attempting to smuggle forty-six dozen parcels of Irish soap into the country, and of attempting to retrieve them by force after they had been seized by two Parkgate customs officers, William Briscoe and William Saunders. Evidence was given that, on 25th January 1757, Briscoe and Saunders, together with other officers, found the soap concealed in the ballast of "The Dublin Packet". The officers loaded the soap into a cart, and carried it to the door of the Custom House, with the intention of securing it in the store there. As they were unloading it, several men, including the accused, rushed them, in an attempt to seize the soap back. According to the Briscoe and Saunders, one of the assailants managed to drive the cart for a distance of seven or eight roods (say, fifty metres) before he was stopped. He seemed to have escaped, but was identified as John Lucas, a mariner belonging to the same ships as Charles Lucas, the accused.

Unfortunately, the records of the trial itself appear to have been lost, so we shall never know whether Charles Lucas, smuggler of soap, came clean.

The great days came to an end in the early nineteenth century. Continued silting made access to Parkgate anchorage increasingly difficult for the packets, and the service was transferred to Liverpool. Although no formal record of when the last packet sailed appears to exist, Philip Sulley, writing in the 1880s, when the event still lay within living memory, stated that it was in 1820.

SOURCES NOT MENTIONED IN THE TEXT

Collins, Greenville "Great Britain Coasting Pilot,1684"

"Chester Chronicle" Various issues.

Craig, Robert "Some Aspects of the Trade and Shipping of the River Dee in the 18th Century" (Transactions of the Historic Society of Lancashire and Cheshire, 1962)

Gamlin, Hilda "Twixt Mersey and Dee" (D. Marples & Co 1897)

"Gore's Directory of Liverpool" (for 1769, 1772, 1774)

Hilditch, Edward "Little Neston Methodist Church Centenary History 1872 - 1972"

Lloyd, G. "The Canalisation of the River Dee in 1737" ("Flintshire Historical Society Journal") xxiii, 1967-8

Mortimer, William "History of the Hundred of Wirral" (1847)

"Pigot's Directory of Cheshire" (for 1822 and 1828)

Place, G. "Theatrical Performances at Parkgate" (Parkgate Society Newsletter, Autumn 1987)

Place, G. "The Rise and Fall of Parkgate, Passenger Port for Ireland 1686-1815" (The Chetham Society, 1994)

Place, G. "This is Parkgate. Its Buildings and their Story" (The Parkgate and District Society, 1979)

Simpson, Colin "Emma, The Life of Lady Hamilton" (Bodley Head, 1983)

Sulley, Philip "The Hundred of Wirral" (Birkenhead, 1889)

Willan, T.S. "Chester and the Navigation of the River Dee 1600-1750" ("Journal of the Chester Archaeological Society" xxxii, 1937)

Chapter Four

The Slump

The half century, or so, that followed the discontinuation of the packet service saw a rapid deterioration in the fortunes of the Neston Area. It was a period when the loss of Neston's most important function, that of a port and communications centre, plunged the Area into a local slump.

Even before the last packet boat had left Parkgate, those who were seeking an outlet from Wirral to the sea began to look towards the Mersey.

In 1835 the New Chester Road was opened, providing a direct link along the north coast of the Peninsula between Chester and Birkenhead, and eliminating the need for passengers travelling between those places to pass through Neston. Little more than a hamlet at the beginning of the century, by the time that plans for Wirral's first railway were being considered, in the 1830's, Birkenhead was a rapidly expanding commercial and shipbuilding town, connected to Liverpool by a steam ferry. That being the case, it is hardly surprising that the planners of The Great Western and The London and North Western Railway Companies settled on the Chester-Birkenhead route for a joint line, which duly opened in 1840. These two new routes deprived the coach services between Chester and Birkenhead, via Neston, of their traffic, and by 1850 they had ceased to exist.

For a few years after the loss of the packet service Parkgate continued to attract summer visitors, but, in the early 1830s, a steady decline set in until, by 1841, a commentator was able to observe,

of late years a new sea bathing place has been created exclusively for the accommodation of the wealthier classes in and about Liverpool, who, having now nearly deserted the once fashionable Parkgate, on the Cheshire coast, gladly availed themselves of the *new establishment to which the emphatic title of New Brighton has been given.**

An idea of the way in which Birkenhead displaced Neston as the most important town on Wirral can be gained from a glance at the population returns for 1801 and 1851.

	1801	1851
Neston Area	2,353	3,578
Birkenhead	110	24,285

The Neston Area's economic problems were aggravated by a sudden and coincidental collapse in the herring fishing industry.

During the eighteenth and early nineteenth centuries vast quantities of herrings had been landed and cured at Parkgate, but this prosperity came to an end in the 1820s. Mortimer, in his book "The History of the Hundred of Wirral" (1847) remarked that,

> *The Fisheries of Leighton* (for modern purposes Parkgate) *were formerly considerable, but are now much neglected.*

The first blow fell in 1820, when the bounties which had been payable to herring fishermen since 1750 were discontinued. About the same time, the fishermen from the ports surrounding the Irish Sea began to face new and formidable competition from Cornish fishermen, who operated in a more efficient manner than the local men.

By 1841, of 235 employed adults in Parkgate, only 13 were fishermen.

The Ness mine remained working (See Appendix B), but it seems to have brought small benefit to the Area generally. To quote Mortimer again,

> *The Village (Ness) is one of the most miserable in the Hundred, consisting of a mere mass of hovels, inhabited by the colliers.*

It was a period when some degree of social, as well as economic change became apparent.

Among other social changes, Congregationalist, Presbyterian, and Roman Catholic congregations were established, thereby extending the breadth of Christian tradition already represented by the Anglican and Methodist churches.

*A.B. Granville "Spas of England" (1841) quoted by G. Place in "The Rise and Fall of Parkgate, Passenger Port for Ireland 1686-1815" (The Chetham Society 1994)

Incidentally, for the Established Church, Neston's boom and slump were almost reflected in the ministry of the two incumbents who held office during these periods.

Prebendary Thomas Ward, Vicar from 1784 to 1828, was an enlightened man, who actively promoted the education and general welfare of his parishioners. Tradition holds that it was Ward who suggested the formation of the Female Friendly Society (see Appendix C), and it was certainly he who revived parish education, which had lapsed with the closure of Windle Hill School, about 1770.

In 1815 he wrote,

> *within the last year we have established a school .... which consists of 80 boys and 50 girls ..... our rooms will not contain a greater number, nor does it seem necessary at present ..... to enlarge them.*

That school stood on part of the site now occupied by the Town Hall.

Ward's successor, Archdeacon Unwin Clarke, Vicar from 1828 to 1847, was a very different sort of man. Clarke, who was also Vicar of Eastham, where he lived, seems to have shown little interest in either of his parishes. For most of his ministry, he left the spiritual care of his flock to his curates, while he hunted with Sir Thomas Stanley's hounds, or imposed harsh punishments in his capacity as a magistrate.

That being the case, it seems probable that it was his Neston curate, Wright Willett, who was the driving force behind the establishment of an infants' school at Little Neston in 1841.

In her book "Twixt Mersey and Dee" (1897) Mrs Hilda Gamlin recounts an entertaining anecdote about Clarke.

> *He was once on his way to sit in his magisterial capacity when he passed a man with a pedlar's stock. The Archdeacon examined his wares, selected a pair of braces, squabbled over the price, and acquired them after splitting the difference. Then he exclaimed. "Now, my man, where is your licence?" High words passed, and, at last, the pedlar produced his paper, which was perfectly regular. The clergyman had not expected this, so in an ill-tempered tone, he said, "I don't want your braces; you can have them back for a shilling", a reduction on his purchase. "Not likely", said the man, "when I can get a cartload for sixpence". "Well, you may have them for ninepence". So the man took them and paid for them and they parted. A woman, who had been watching the transaction,*

Old Parkgate, Cheshire

9. Parkgate 1840. Drawing from a contemporary, anonymous painting by an anonymous artist.
(Collection Ian Boumphrey)

*told the pedlar the name of the Archdeacon, and that he was going
to Birkenhead to attend a meeting of magistrates. The man asked
her to go with him to Birkenhead, where he took out a summons
against the Archdeacon for peddling without a licence, and used
the woman as a witness to the sale of the braces for ninepence. He
served the summons on Clarke as he sat on the bench, had the case
heard there and then, and obtained a conviction with fine and costs.*

Without doubt, the most significant event, both economically and socially,
to occur during this period was the sale by the Mostyn Family of their
lands in the Area, together with their other Cheshire lands.

The last male member of the family which had owned most of Great Neston
and all of Parkgate since 1672, Sir Thomas Mostyn, died unmarried in
1831. The estate passed to the husband of his eldest surviving sister, Sir
Thomas Swymmer Champreys Bart., and Sir Thomas's Mostyn's five sisters
went to the High Court of Chancery to claim the £10,000 each, which their
father, Sir Roger Mostyn, had bequeathed them in his will.

It would appear that these legacies had not been paid by 1838, when an
attempt was made to sell various Cheshire properties, including some at
Neston and Parkgate, in,

*The interest of the assignees of Sir Thomas Swymmer Mostyn
Champneys, Bart., an insolvent debtor in estates devised by the will
of the late Sir Roger Mostyn Bart.*

The sale was advertised to take place,

*At Garraway's Coffee House, Change Alley, Cornhill, London, on
Saturday, 19th November 1838.*

The properties being offered as one lot.

The sale failed and the same Neston/Parkgate properties were again offered
for sale by the Mostyn Family, and successfully auctioned, in 1849.

Sir Thomas Champneys died on the 21st November 1839, and the
administration of the estate passed to his nephew by marriage, Edward
Mostyn.

Edward was the son another of Sir Thomas Mostyn's daughters and her
husband, Edward Lloyd, first Baron Mostyn. Heir to both the title and the
Mostyn estates, he adopted the surname Mostyn by royal licence when he
took control of the Estate.

As administrator of the Estate, Edward inherited severe financial problems.
In addition to raising the £50,000 needed to pay his mother and aunts, he

10. An old print depicting the north side of the Cross as it was about 1850.
Of those shown, the only building still standing is the tall one with the arched window in the background.

found himself faced with the problem of restoring solvency to an estate that was £100,000 in debt.

That being so, he decided to sell his Cheshire estates, including his lands and properties in Neston and Parkgate.

The auction of 1,500 acres in Great Neston, Parkgate, Leighton, Thornton Hough and Hinderton took place over six days in June 1849 at the Mostyn Arms Hotel, Parkgate. Possibly profiting from the experience of the 1838 Sale, when Sir Thomas Champneys had failed in his attempt to sell some four hundred properties as one lot, Edward offered the various properties, comprising the bulk - but not quite all - of his estate in the Area, as 284 separate lots.

Among the consequences of the Sale, and yet another blow to the economy of the Area, was the discontinuation of Neston Fair, which had been held three times a year, and the weekly market, both of which had been held at the Cross since they had been authorised by a royal charter granted to Sir Roger Mostyn and his heirs, as Lords of the Manor of Great Neston, in 1728. With no Mostyn as Lord of the Manor there could be no fair or market.

The Mostyn Sale was the first, and biggest, of a number of sales which broke up the manorial estates in the Neston Area. The Cottingham Family sold its two-fifths share of Little Neston in 1851. The Earl of Shrewsbury sold his three-fifths of Little Neston in 1913, and his Neston lands from 1911 to 1913. The Stanley Family sold off their Ness estate about 1895.

SOURCES NOT MENTIONED IN THE TEXT

Chambers, S. Hilditch, E. Place, G. and others "Neston 1840 - 1940" (Burton and South Wirral Local History Society, 1996)

Cheshire Records Office. "Inquiry into the State of Parish Education"(1815) C.R.O. EDA 6/9/36

Cokayne G.E. "Complete Baronetage, Vol 5".

Mostyn Estate Sale Catalogue and Map 1849 (In private hands)

Place, G. "The Rise and Fall of Parkgate, Passenger Port for Ireland 1686 - 1815" (Chetham Society, 1994)

Poster and Schedule advertising the 1838 Mostyn Sale. (In Neston Library Local History Collection)

Chapter Five

Off with the Old; on with the New

The old landlords had leased almost all their holdings on an annual basis, which was the usual term under the manorial system in Cheshire.

While this custom of yearly tenancies may have had some advantages for the landlords, it did nothing to encourage tenants to improve their homes or holdings. Agriculture in the Neston Area seems to have been conducted in a half-hearted manner, with small regard for the improved farming methods developed elsewhere during the eighteenth century.

Not only did the sale of the Mostyn lands - and, in due course, those of the other manorial landlords - allow many more residents to own their homes and farms, and provide a potent incentive for them to make improvements, it afforded them a measure of independence which had not previously been possible. It was a portent of better times ahead.

But not for the community as a whole. At least, not immediately.

In manorial times local government had been in the hands of two authorities: the Manorial Courts and the Parish Vestry, each with its own, complementary, powers and duties. The Mostyn Sale, with its associated withdrawal of the manorial system, had deprived the former Manors of Great Neston and of Leighton and Thornton of the Manorial Courts, and left the responsibility for the administration of the town completely in the hands of the Parish Vestry, a body that was, in 1849, empowered to exercise only one of the former powers of the Manorial Courts. In 1842 parish vestries had acquired the manorial courts' duty and power to appoint unpaid, part-time, township constables - in reality the responsibility of administering an antiquated policing system that had already been rendered obsolete in Cheshire by the Cheshire Police Act of 1829.

By the end of the 1850s the Vestry had been invested with some of the other duties and powers previously exercised by the Manorial Courts, but, even if it had acquired them all, it would still have been unable to meet the needs of the community to move with the increasingly fast-changing times.

As far as policing was concerned, the problem of establishing a regular, professional, police presence in the Area was solved by action at County level. The Act of 1829, and a number of subsequent, supplementary, Acts made the establishment of a paid police force compulsory throughout the County and, in 1865, a building housing a police station and magistrates' court was built in Park Street, on a site behind the present Methodist Church.

It was not in the power of the Vestry to do anything about the state of squalor in which many parts of Great Neston and the surrounding villages existed at that time. In 1886 a correspondent to the "Chester Chronicle" described sanitary conditions in the Neston of some twenty years previously in the following terms:

It had neither sewers in the streets nor adequate drainage to its dwellings, while its foetid ashpits and excramentitious receptacles in all sorts of wretched constructions were to be found that would help in the germination of diseases. The town was then without an adequate supply of pure water. What was required for culinary and other household purposes was collected from brooks, ditches, ponds and pits , stagnant receptacles wherein zotifers wriggled and lively polywogs desported.....the people of the lower classes were the most susceptible to contract disease by reason of the debauched, dirty, and drunken habits they led. The very air in those days was impregnated with malaria that rose from the foetid receptacles of filth that everywhere seethed and festered in the sun.

It was all so unnecessary. The means to deal with this situation had became available with the passing of The Local Government Act of 1858, which allowed communities to elect a local board of health. These local boards were empowered to raise a rate, and pass bye-laws to: secure a good water supply, an efficient system of sewerage, adequate street lighting and cleaning, and make road improvements.

There was, however, no legal obligation to establish such boards, and, although efforts were made by the Vicar, Richard Gleadowe, and others, to promote the formation of a Neston Board, most of those who were already paying rates to the Parish Vestry were opposed to the notion of a second rate-raising body. That being so, nothing was done until the town was faced by a major crisis.

In September 1866, the Area was struck by an outbreak of the cholera which was sweeping the country. The disease had already claimed some 2,000 victims in Liverpool, and one local tradition holds that it arrived in the Neston Area with a Liverpool woman, who came to Parkgate to convalesce. She, the story goes, gave her linen to a servant in her lodging house to wash, and, in doing so, passed the disease on to the servant and the landlady. All three - landlady, servant, and guest - died.

The disease spread rapidly, and at least eleven people died within the first week.

For some, death came with terrifying swiftness. Michael O'Loughlin, a 66-year-old tailor from Parkgate Road, developed the first symptoms at six o'clock one evening and was dead by 9 a.m. the next day. James Smith, a 29-year-old grocer on the Cross, died within seven hours.

To meet the crisis, a committee was formed to carry into effect the provisions of the Nuisance and Disease Prevention Acts. Prominent among its six members were the Vicar, Dick Gleadowe, and Christopher Bushell, a Liverpool wine merchant and local benefactor, who had settled in Neston in 1856.

The Committee held meetings with Dr. David Russell, the town Medical Officer, every morning of the epidemic, to review the situation, and to decide on the measures needed to meet any developments.

Dr Russell was provided with an assistant, a nurse, and a horse, and two cottages off Mill Street were converted for use as a temporary hospital. In accordance with the provisions of the Disease Prevention Act, all soiled linen and bedding used by those suffering from Cholera was burned, and chloride of lime was spread in the streets as a disinfectant.

The epidemic lasted three weeks, or so, and claimed thirty-seven lives in Neston and Parkgate, and a further seven in Little Neston.

With the cholera threat over for the time being, Russell, Gleadowe, Bushell, and several other prominent residents. began to plan the only effective defence against further outbreaks: an adequate, clean, piped, water supply.

There had, in fact, been a good source of pure water in Neston since the middle of the eighteenth century. In 1749 a small waterworks, based on a well, was opened on the site where Derek Massey's butcher's shop now stands, at the junction of Raby Road and High Street. Water was piped to a number of houses in the town, and it was also sold by the jugful at the waterworks.

During the cholera epidemic Dr. Russell wrote,

> .....*with few exceptions, the inhabitants of Neston use the water supplied by the waterworks...*

In this, however, he was almost certainly mistaken, and the "Chester Chronicle" correspondent nearer the truth of the matter. In those far-off days of general ignorance concerning matters of hygiene, and when poverty was widespread, it seems certain that many of those living in the Area would, indeed, have obtained their water from brooks, ditches, and the like, rather than pay for it. If it had not been so, Christopher Bushell would not have paid for a public well to be sunk on the Cross in 1865, to be a source of free, good, water for the town. Unfortunately, this well soon became contaminated by seepage through the sandstone bedrock from the horse manure which collected in the streets, and from the ashpits, middens, pigsties, stables, and slaughterhouses that were scattered among the houses.

In 1866 the situation concerning water supplies was, therefore, as the epidemic had demonstrated, highly dangerous.

That being so, a public meeting was called in March 1867, to discuss the formation of a Local Board of Health. It was a stormy occasion. Memories of the cholera outbreak had begun to fade, and there were those to whom the prospect of paying for a good water supply and a modern sewage system did not appeal. In the event, the proposal to establish the Board was adopted, but there were sections of the community among whom resentment continued to fester for years.

The Neston and Parkgate Local Board of Health met for the first time on 30th August 1867 in the Church School (now Scholars' Court), under the chairmanship of Christopher Bushell, and its first act was to declare a rate of 6d in the £1.

In the twenty-seven years of its existence Neston Local Board implemented several important measures which secured a sound basis for the modernisation of the Area. They included the construction of a waterworks on much the same site of the present waterworks in Little Neston - the old waterworks having been judged to be inadequate - together with a network of pipes to carry the water to buildings and standpipes; the installation of a sewage plant in a field off Church Lane, together with an extensive system of sewers; and the provision of street lighting.

Private enterprise also made important contributions to the general modernisation of the Neston Area.

11. Neston Cross c1870. Note the old White Horse Inn, which was demolished in 1877, and the winding wheel of the old public well, presented to the town by Christopher Bushell in 1865.

12. The former retort house of Neston Gas Works still stands off Church Lane.

13. Neston High Street about 1900. Built in the mid-1600s, the stone barn on the right of the picture is one of the oldest buildings still standing in the town.

14. Photo taken just a little further down the High Street than Illustration 13, and about ten years later. Notice John George Lee's shop. For many years Lee's was something of a Neston institution. In addition to providing all the services expected of a High Street chemist, before the arrival of the first dentist in the town, about 1915, John Lee extracted teeth, without the benefit of anaesthetic and at a fee of a shilling (5 pence) a tooth. After his death, his son, George Brian Lee, continued the business until 1971. The shop, together with the rest of the block in which it stood, was demolished in 1973.

15. Parkgate, 1880. The building in the foreground was "The George" inn during the eighteenth and early nineteeth centuries. From 1819 to 1855 it remained in business as "The Mostyn Arms" hotel. The building survives as part of Mostyn House School, but its facade has been much altered. (Collection Ian Boumphrey)

16. Ness c.1900.

46

Gld-Inn Little Neston

17. The Old Royal Oak at Little Neston stood on the site now occupied by the present Royal Oak. Described by Philip Sulley in 1889 as "......a very ancient, rambling, thatched structure of one storey, exceedingly picturesque", it was burnt down in 1901. The large granite boulder in the foreground was unearthed by Neston Council workmen about 1895, and placed on Little Neston Green. Some fifteen years later the Council decided to break it up to make road foundations. William Hesketh Lever (later Lord Leverhulme) intervened, and offered the Council an equivalent weight of macadam in exchange for the stone. The deal made, he placed it in the sunken garden at Thornton Manor, where it may still be seen.

Indeed, it was private enterprise that contributed the single most important factor to the economic revival of the Area, in the shape of the Hooton to Parkgate Railway.

Its route now familiar as that of the Wirral Country Park, the single track was built as a branch line from the Chester-Birkenhead Railway, to afford the two Railway Companies which operated the line access to the steam coal from the projected Ness Mine, and with some idea of providing a connection with the Parkgate-North Wales Ferry Service. In the event, the Ferry Service was discontinued before the line became operational (see Appendix D).

The line, which opened on Monday, 10th October 1866, ended at Parkgate, with stations at Willaston, Neston, and Parkgate.

Twenty years later, the London and North Western and Great Western Joint Board extended the line to West Kirkby.

It was the coming of the Railway that determined the present residential character of Neston-cum-Parkgate, and south-west Wirral generally. Its construction was followed by a rapid growth in the villages along its route, as people who worked in Liverpool or Birkenhead realised that they could now live on the quieter Dee coast of the Peninsula, and commute to work. This growth was reflected in the census returns for the years before and after the line was opened. In the thirty years from 1841 to 1871 the population of the Neston Area increased by approximately 9%, but in the following thirty years, those roughly coinciding with the first thirty years of the Railway, the population of the Area increased by 124%.

Thereafter there was a fall in the rate of increase, but it remained vigorous until well into the 1970s.

From the time that the line was opened until the last few years of its existence, in the 1950s, commuter traffic between Neston, and the other stations along the line, and Birkenhead was considerable.

The advent of the Railway transformed the character of the Neston Area, stimulated expansion, and, with its potential for providing rapid access to markets, it kindled resurgences in local farming and fishing.

Not only did the Railway stimulate the expansion of the Neston Area and promote economic activity, it provided the means to meet the needs of the growing population. Before the Second World War the bulk of the traffic into and out of the Area was carried by rail. Inward traffic included such diverse items as barrels of beer from Burton-on-Trent, road stone from the quarries of North Wales, manure from Birkenhead Lairage, and seed potatoes from Scotland. The late Albert Manning, who worked at Neston Station from 1923 to 1932, remembered an entire circus, complete with elephants, arriving by rail. Outward traffic included coal from the Ness Mine, shellfish from Parkgate, and livestock.

The local police must have been particularly thankful for the existence of the Railway on 8th April 1880 - Election Day - when there was almost a breakdown in law and order.

It was the first election to have been held in the town for forty years. The sun shone, flags danced in the spring breeze, the church bells rang, and in the streets people flaunted rosettes to proclaim their political allegiances: yellow for Liberal and blue for Conservative. Drink flowed in the pubs.

48

18. (left) 1907. Grocer John Pearson stands outside his shop, with two of his sons, Dick (wearing cap) and George. The shop stood on approximately the same site as that now occupied by the Sue Ryder Charity Shop, but it projected further out into the street. It was demolished as part of a road-widening scheme in 1928.
(Collection Ted Pearson)

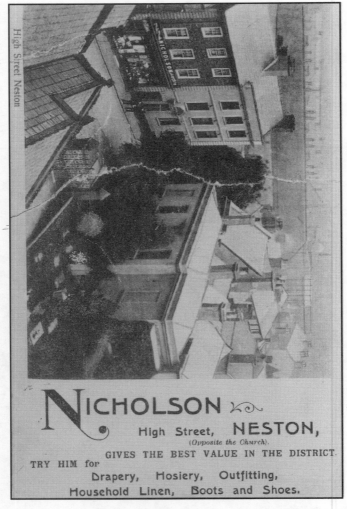

19. *An unusual and interesting photograph taken from the Parish Church tower about 1910, and used to illustrate an advertisement for Nicholson's shop. The building on the immediate right was bought by the Church in 1920, as a home for the senior curate, and renamed "Church House". It was demolished as part of a road-widening scheme in the late 1920s, and the Parish Hall now occupies part of the site. Until 1920 curates had lived in the white building - the original "Church House" - on the other side of the street (now Gittin's shop). The former Nicolson's shop is now occupied by an estate agency.*

20. Ness. The village celebrates Coronation Day 1911.

21. Coronation Day in Neston, 1911. Note the Boy Scouts with their round hats and staves. They are members of the Parish Church Troop. (Collection Ian Boumphrey

22. Neston Church Scouts Football Team 1911-12.
Back Row from left: George Oxton; Jack Henderson; Harry Maylor. Middle
Row from left: Joe Jones; not known; Jim Harris; not known; Jody Tudor;
Tommy Tudor (coach, with cap and towel). None of the front row known.

23. 1914, Parkgate and the Denna Gutter. For centuries the Denna Gutter ran
straight down from Denhall and parallel with the coast. It was not until the 1930s
that it wandered off, on its present course, towards the Point of Ayr.

The possibility of trouble had not been overlooked by the Authorities. An Assistant Superintendent Plant had been drafted from Birkenhead to take charge of police operations for the day, and to provide the election experience that the local Sergeant, Jim O'Donnell, and his men lacked.

It proved to have been a wise precaution. At about two o'clock sporadic fighting broke out at various points in the High Street. This early skirmishing appears to have been non-political in character, being occasioned by such gentlemen as Frank McLevy, who threw down his hat, and defied all comers to tread on it, and William Millan, who accepted the challenge with the words, "I will have a go."

At about 2.30 p.m. however, the appearance of a group of men leading a lamb beribboned in Conservative blue from the direction of Parkgate provoked something approaching a crisis.

Within minutes, the brawl that started when they were set upon by Liberal supporters had spread and developed into a street battle involving dozens of individual encounters.

It was with considerable difficulty that the handful of local policemen managed to separate the factions and to impose an uneasy truce on the town. Despite the scale of the fighting, they made no arrests at that stage, confining themselves to restraining and warning the combatants.

Aware that he and his men had won nothing but a breathing space, Plant telegraphed Birkenhead for reinforcements.

Thanks to the co-operation and fast work of the railway management, the police authorities were able to get thirty extra constables from Birkenhead to Neston within the hour.

They were needed. Throughout the afternoon tension increased steadily. Scattered fighting occurred, and a number of arrests were made.

As daylight faded, the police found themselves confronted by a howling, stone-throwing mob, estimated by Plant to number over a thousand.

The police drew their batons and charged the rioters, who scattered and retreated to neighbouring alleyways, from where they maintained a steady barrage of missiles on Plant's men. Some broke into nearby gardens and tore branches from trees, the better to come to close quarters with the police.

It was at this point that Plant sent to Ashfield Hall for local magistrate Uvedale Corbett to read the Riot Act - the Act that allowed the police to call on the Army for assistance.

Fortunately for all concerned, Corbett arrived during a lull in the fighting that enabled him to address the rioters. Standing at the Cross, brandishing his copy of the Act, he warned them of the serious consequences that could follow if he read it, and appealed to them to go home.

It worked. Slowly at first, and then more and more rapidly, the crowd melted away until the streets were empty. By ten o'clock Plant considered the situation to be stable enough for him to stand all his men down, except those who would normally have been on duty.

Considering the scale of the disturbances, surprisingly few rioters appeared in court. Only seven men and one woman were convicted of being drunk and disorderly, and were fined either one pound or ten shillings, according to the gravity of their offences, with the option of fourteen days or seven days hard labour respectively.

A third railway station was provided for the Area when a new line, which had been built from Seacombe to Wrexham by The Manchester, Sheffield, and Lincolnshire Railway Company, was opened in 1896.

Other private enterprise contributions were made to the modernisation of the Neston Area by The Neston and Parkgate Gas Company, which built a gasworks off Church Lane in 1882; The National Telephone Company, which installed the Area's first telephones in 1889; and The Neston Town Hall Company, which built the Town Hall during the period 1888-9, the Local Board, presumably, not having the power to raise a rate for the purpose.

In 1894 the Local Board was dissolved and replaced by "Neston-cum-Parkgate Urban District Council", a new type of authority which had been sanctioned by the Local Government Act of that year, and one that was invested with wider powers than the old Board.

Under the direction of this new body, Neston bustled its way into the twentieth century with the construction of an up-to-date sewage disposal plant at Moorside in 1902-03, and with the erection of a public library.

Planned as Neston's memorial to Queen Victoria, the Library was built in 1907 on land given by Mrs Russell, widow of Dr David Russell, and with aid of a grant from the American industrialist Andrew Carnegie. With the provision of a library service, Neston-cum-Parkgate became the smallest library authority in the country, a distinction it retained even when it was reformed with an extended area of jurisdiction as "Neston Urban District Council" in 1933.

Most of the churches now in use were built or rebuilt between the middle of the nineteenth century and the outbreak of the First World War in 1914.

St Winifred's Roman Catholic Church was originally built as a church school in 1841. In the event, there was so little support for the school that the project was temporarily postponed and, in 1843, the building was converted for use as a chapel. A number of extensions have since been made to the original building.

The fact that Methodism was established in the Neston Area in the mid-eighteenth century has already been mentioned in Chapter 3. Nationally, the early nineteenth century saw a number of divisions appear in the Methodist Movement, and, until the various branches were re-united in 1932, both Wesleyan Methodism and Primitive Methodism were represented in the Area. In 1872 the Primitive Methodists built the present Little Neston Church, and, in 1912, the Wesleyan Methodists built the Church on the corner of Park Street and Liverpool Road in Neston.

The United Reformed Church was built as a Presbyterian Church in 1884.

The years 1874-75 saw the almost complete demolition of the old Parish Church - judged to be unsafe and beyond restoration - and its replacement by a much bigger building. Of the old church only the tower was retained, having been restored at the turn of the seventeenth and eighteenth centuries. The Vicar, Dick Gleadowe, made use of a trowel that was discovered in the old masonry to lay the first stone of the present building.

The wooden predecessor of the present St Michael's Church at Little Neston was built in 1913.

It was during the second half of the nineteenth century that the Anglican parish was pared down to its present boundaries, and, incidentally, the area which is the subject of this book. Four of the old parish townships were either used as the basis of a new parish or formed part of a new parish: Ledsham was incorporated into the parish of Capenhurst in 1859; Willaston became a parish in 1865, and Thornton Hough and Raby together were amalgamated to form the Parish of Thornton Hough in 1869.

The period between the middle of the nineteenth century and 1914 was also notable for a wave of school building.

Father James Pemberton revived the plan for a Catholic school in 1856, when a gift of £500 provided the financial means to build a new one close to the church. Opened in January 1857, it is possible that this second school was rendered viable by a policy of admitting Protestant children. The late Mrs. Mary Speed (nee Lee) estimated that when she attended St

Winifred's School, from 1906 to 1909, about half the pupils were Protestant.

By the 1850s, the Church of England school building, opened in 1814, was in an advanced state of dilapidation, and too small to accommodate the rapidly-expanding school population.

That being so, the Parish embarked on an ambitious programme of school building.

A new school was built in Liverpool Road, and opened in January 1859. Known locally throughout its existence as, "The Top School", this new building was designed to accommodate 266 pupils.

A 60-pupil infants' school was built at Parkgate, and opened in 1860.

In 1870 the church infants' school in Little Neston was replaced by a new, all-age, elementary school at Ness Holt.

A council school, established in 1905, was housed in temporary quarters at Little Neston until the new, purpose-designed, buildings on Burton Road were ready in 1909.

The first Headteacher of the Council School, Robert W. Jones, seems to have been a colourful character. A smallish man, who wore his hair cropped Prussian fashion and who habitually sported plus-fours, "Taffy's" otherwise inflexible discipline was obviously tempered by the knowledge that many of the older pupils had early-morning family duties to fulfil that sometimes made them late for school. Instead of a grilling, or worse, latecomers likely to be in that situation were usually greeted with a well-worn quip. For example, those from Parkgate - where there was still a good beach - were liable to be met with, "Sand in the clock again?" Possibly emboldened by the fact that he commanded a second income from a shop he owned at Ness, Jones was never afraid to voice his frequent disagreements with the school governors.

Throughout the nineteenth century and until the Second World War, there were a number of private schools in the Area. Some, like Dr Riddock's School, in Little Neston, and Anne Pakenham-Walsh's School at the Cross flourished for fifty years, and more; others were very short-lived. Most existed for a decade or two. Mostyn House School, which opened at Parkgate in 1855, is the longest-surviving of the private schools, but, having always drawn the majority of its pupils from places outside the Area, it is rather a school in Parkgate than of it.

At the outbreak of the First World War, then, Neston offered all the services and amenities that could reasonably have been expected of a town at that time, except mains electricity. For that Nestonians had to wait until 1928.

SOURCES NOT MENTIONED IN THE TEXT

Chambers, S. "Neston and the Cholera" (Neston Civic Society Bulletin, 20th October 1986)

Chambers, S., Hilditch, E., Place, G., and others. "Neston 1840-1940" (The Burton and South Wirral Local History Society, 1996)

Hilditch, E. "Little Neston Methodist Church, Centenary History 1872-1972"

Manning, Albert, the late. (clerk, Neston GWR/LMS Station 1933-39) Author's interview with re. Neston Station.

Merseyside Railway History Group. "The Hooton to West Kirby Branch Line and the Wirral Way." (Metropolitan Borough of Wirral, 1982)

Peters, Jim, the late (Former pupil Neston Council School) Author's recorded interview with.

Speed (nee Lee) Mary, the late (former pupil St Winifred's School and Neston Council School), Author's recorded interview with.

Sulley, Philip "The Hundred of Wirral" (1889)

Various editions of "The Chester Chronicle" and "The Birkenhead Advertiser"

Chapter Six

1914-1939

When the new Wirral Battalion of the Cheshire Regiment mustered at Chester Castle on 5th September 1914 - just a month after the outbreak of the First World War - there were fourteen men from the Neston Area in its ranks. Over the following four years a steady stream of men left to serve with the forces, and by the Armistice, in November 1918, over three hundred Nestonians were wearing, or had worn, the King's Uniform.

For a few months after the outbreak of war there was a lull, during which time those who remained at home could only await developments. The news of the first Zeppelin raids on the country, in early 1915, created a demand for dark material with which to make black-out curtains, and prompted the Committee of the Female Friendly Society (See Appendix C) to cancel the Annual Walk for the duration of hostilities.

Neston Institute - now the Civic Hall - was converted into a temporary Red Cross military hospital, and Parkgate Convalescent Home, which stood on part of the site now occupied by Deeside Court, was converted into a temporary Red Cross military convalescent home. The sight of the blue-trousered patients soon became familiar about the town, and many were welcomed into local homes.

A small munitions factory was established in sheds at "Leighton Court", the home of wealthy cotton broker W. E. Whinnery, and a recruiting office was opened at the Town Hall in November 1915.

In personal terms, the news from the war zones was usually bad. The late Annie Johnson remarked that hardly a week passed without news of someone's son, brother, or husband being killed or wounded.

In May 1918 Neston learned that Christopher Bushell - grandson of the benefactor whose generosity is commemorated by the Cross monument - had been awarded the Victoria Cross.

A lieutenant-colonel in the Royal West Surrey Regiment, Bushell was severely wounded in the head on 23rd March, while personally commanding "C" Company of his division, on a sector of the Front to the north of Tergnier, France. He continued to walk about in front of his troops, and refused to have the wound dressed until the line was reorganised in a strong position to meet a turning movement of the enemy. He died of his wound on 8th August 1918.

During the course of the First World War the Neston Area lost ninety-one men.

For many Nestonians, as for people elsewhere, the inter-war years brought hard times. The local unemployment problem precipitated by the run-down years of the Little Neston Mine and then its final closure in 1927, the national crisis of the General Strike, and the international catastrophe of the Slump, were all reflected in a shortage of money and the things that money could buy.

Lilian Jones (nee Williams) recalls an occasion in the mid-thirties, when she and her brother - both of junior school age - squabbled over who should have a piece of brown paper litter, which they had spotted wedged in a hedge, to line their well-worn shoes.

Not that hard times had been unknown before 1919. For the unemployed and those in poorly-paid occupations Life had always been hard, but the high general level of unemployment experienced during the twenties and thirties reduced many more folk to penny-pinching.

Many of the new poor turned to the means whereby the long-term poor had, probably for centuries, supplemented their incomes. Means that were many and varied.

As an area that boasted far more countryside than it does to-day, and located on an estuary that comprised both marshland and tidal reaches, 1920s/30s Neston offered much in the way of seasonal work and free food.

In season, it offered blackberries from the hedgerows, mushrooms and rabbits from the fields, water-cress from the Broad Brook at Ness, sampkin (see Illustration 28) and shellfish from the mud-flats and sandbanks, flukes(flounders) and grey mullet from the tides, gulls' and ducks' eggs from the marsh, and harvest work on the farms.

Many of the wild crops were not just gathered by Nestonians for their own use. So abundant were yields that, even in relatively poor years, it was always possible to collect a surplus for sale at Birkenhead or Liverpool Market.

24. *During the First World War, the Institute (now the Civic Hall) was pressed into service as a temporary Red Cross military hospital. Here some of the patients pose with a nurse and a few local children.*
(Collection Ian Boumphrey)

25. *1920. Charlie Bushell stands outside his shop with his six-year-old daughter Margery. Carson Print Services now occupy the shop.*
(Collection Mollie Wright)

26. Jack Whiteway (left), Manager of the British Argentine Meat shop, pictured in 1925 with his daughter Margaret and his assistant, Jack Evans. Derek Massey's business now occupies the shop. (Collection Arnold Whiteway.)

27. Neston Bible Class Football Team 1921-22.
Back row, from left: Rev Horatio Sharples (Curate); Bill Jervis; Tom Bridson; Jack Chrimes; Bill Anyon; Bill Pearson; Jack Mellor; Bill Roberts (Manager). Front row, from left: Archie Scally; Jack Anyon; Sam Smith; not known; not known; Harry Williams; Joe Mealor. (Collection Ted Pearson.)

61

28. (opposite) Family gathering sampkin on the Dee Estuary. Known elsewhere as "samphire" or "glasswort", until the advent of allotments and large cottage gardens, between the wars, this estuary plant was an important crop for many of the area's working folk.

Harvested between May and August, sampkin has no woody base, it looks almost like a desert plant, albeit a smooth one. Young plants can be eaten raw, but more mature ones need a brief cooking. They can be added to soups and sauces, or used as a vegetable with a main meal.

Sampkin can be pickled in vinegar, so those who gathered this free crop could continue to enjoy it throughout the winter months.

During the season, some Nestonians supplemented their income by taking quantities of sampkin to Birkenhead Market - by horse and trap, or, more commonly, by hand cart - where there was always a good demand for it. (Collection Harry Jones)

29. A stormy day at Parkgate in the mid-1930s.

30. Parkgate Baths c1930.
(Collection Ian Boumphrey)

For all that, such casual and seasonal activities could not compensate for the lack of a regular wage. With plenty of surplus labour available, casual work earned only low wages, and seasonal crops - because they so often created a glut - brought only low prices.

That being so, for much of the inter-war period, the queues at the Dole Office in Brook Street and, later, in Chester Road, were long. Many stood about the streets hoping for the chance of employment, and it was common to see two or three men on bicycles following a wagon load of timber or bricks, to find out where the work was taking place, so they could ask for a job. Equally common was the sight of children slopping round in worn-out and cast-off adult boots.

Both as individuals and in groups, some of the more fortunate residents tried to help the less fortunate.

For example, during the winter months Mrs Arthur Bulley made frequent visits to Ness Holt School in her 'Model T' Ford mini-bus, with hot soup for the pupils. It was the nearest thing to a meal that some of them enjoyed

64

during the school day. At the same time, she would make a mental note of any pupil whose clothes betrayed extraordinary hardship, and then find some diplomatic way to help his or her family.

In 1926 a number of prosperous local residents established a Council of Social Service, to be funded by public subscription. They included Mrs Bulley, John Larden Williams, a solicitor, and Lionel Barber, a merchant. Its aims included: establishing contact with the various existing public, private, and church bodies already involved in various aspect of social welfare work, in an attempt to prevent duplication and overlapping; investigating individual cases of hardship, and providing appropriate assistance; helping the young in their work and leisure, in particular by providing playing fields; and helping those who wanted to emigrate.

The Council established a number of committees each charged with realising a particular aspect of these general aims. Among the committees which existed at various times were a Clothing Committee, which organised a system for the supply of second-hand clothing and footwear to the poor; an Emigration Committee, to assist those wishing to seek better lives overseas; and a Playing Fields and Amenities Committee.

The Council placed much emphasis, wherever possible, on helping the needy to help themselves.

One expression of this policy was the creation of an Allotments Committee. Until the inter-war years, many Neston residents lived in terraced houses - most of them now demolished or converted into business premises - which lacked gardens. By buying a large field off Burton Road and dividing it into vegetable plots, which it leased out at nominal rents, the Committee afforded people, who would not otherwise be able to do so, the opportunity to grow some of their own food.

The Unemployed Work Centre was another expression of the Council of Social Service's enthusiasm for self-help. Located in a building off West Vale, the Centre housed workshops where joinery and boot repair skills were taught, and where materials were sold at reduced prices.

In 1928 The Council established the Neston and Parkgate Housing Society to help to provide decent rented accommodation for those in the Area who were still living in squalor. By raising interest-free loans from some of the more prosperous residents, and with the help of a government subsidy, the Society was able to build a considerable number of houses on Liverpool, Burton, and Marshlands Roads. Much emphasis was placed on the provision of large gardens to encourage tenants to grow vegetables

31. Open air drawing class at Ness Holt School.

From the left:

Back row: Harold Swift (open collar); Ron Smith (kneeling); Cyril Jones (dark grey-looking jersey); George Peers (lying down).

Middle row: Bill Ashington (Dark hair/tie); Les Pinnegar (white-looking jersey); Jim Young (grey-looking jersey/drawing pad); Herbert Hulley (pad on knee); Wilf Cotterell (Holding pencil upright).

Front row: Harold Williams (shirt sleeves/crossed legs); Les Lewis (leaning forwards); Arthur Johnson; Les Peters (with glasses); Tommy Baxter (lying down); Walter Young; George Peers (lying down); John Monighan (kneeling up); Eddy Hand (extreme right).

and keep hens. The Society is still very active, and by building "The Court" off Marshlands Road, it became the first housing concern in Cheshire to provide sheltered accommodation for the elderly.

Neston Council, too, built houses in various parts of the Area, and, despite the difficult financial climate, a considerable amount of speculative housing development took place.

In 1930 the Telephone Exchange moved from the house in Liverpool Road where it had been located since the local system had been installed, to the present purpose-built building, and in 1939, the old Police Station in Park Street was replaced by the present building.

It would, therefore, be a mistake to visualise inter-war Neston as presenting a picture of unrelieved gloom.

In fact, Parkgate was enjoying a degree of relative prosperity.

In 1923 the Headmaster of Mostyn House School, A. G. Grenfell, opened a new, open-air swimming pool at the far end of the North Parade, using the sea-water from the Estuary. The bath was 335 feet long, and the water shelved from three feet six at the shallow end to seven feet six at the deep end. (Illustration 30)

Although Grenfell built the pool primarily for the use of his pupils, he also opened it to the general public. In fact, he depended on his patrons' entry money to meet its running costs. On one occasion, at least, when receipts fell below his expectations he employed low cunning to restore them: he wrote a letter to a newspaper, under a false name, complaining about the indecent swimsuits that had been in evidence at Parkgate Baths during the previous weekend.

It was rarely that he needed to resort to such subterfuges. Parkgate Baths were very popular, and on fine days in the summer, they drew crowds from miles around. Every Sunday afternoon during the 1920s a three-piece band played for the patrons from two p.m. until four. Mrs Nessie Williams, who regularly played in it, recalls that it always started with a waltz followed by a foxtrot. At some time during the 1930s the band was replaced by records and a loud-speaker.

In 1930 Grenfell was able to add a second, children's pool. Half the length of the adult pool, it shelved from a depth of two feet to four feet six inches.

Two gastronomic delights that also drew day trippers to Parkgate were Nicholl's ice cream and the local shrimps.

There was something very special about the ice-cream that was made by the Thomas family, who presided at Nicholl's. Visitors and local alike flocked to buy it, and to enjoy the view from the balcony over the shops as they ate it.

Parkgate shrimps were - and, to an extent, still are - famous throughout the north-west, with a fame that supported a considerable number of shops and cafes.

For much of the inter-war period Parkgate still boasted a good beach for visitors and locals to enjoy, and the wide expanses of sand that stretched for miles in front of the sea wall encouraged some adventurous spirits to build and operate sand yachts.

The great end-of-season attraction at Parkgate was the annual charity fireworks display. Presented by the Headmasters of Mostyn House School - first A. G. Grenfell and then, from 1933, his son, A.M.D. Grenfell - it packed the Parade with spectators.

The fireworks were arranged about two hundred yards out on the sandbanks, on a day when the tides would not ruin the show. As dusk fell, the School's carillon, played by a Belgian virtuoso, invited to Parkgate for the occasion, rang out to invite and entertain the gathering crowd.

The show began when it was dark. It lasted for about an hour, and, from all accounts, it was always memorable. While the fireworks played, collectors passed among the crowd soliciting donations for the year's charity.

Although it was the outbreak of the Second World War that brought the fireworks displays to an end, there were clear signs that Parkgate's days as a port and resort were all but finished. Silting had continued apace. The local fishermen (See Appendix A) had begun to work from Heswall, only bringing their boats back on the highest tides for painting and other maintenance work. A layer of mud had settled over the sand, and the first tufts of spartina grass had appeared by the South Slipway.

SOURCES NOT MENTIONED IN THE TEXT

Author's own memories

Benyon nee Carr, Vistula (Former telephone operator). Author's conversations with re telephone exchange.

Bushell, Liz. Author's conversations with, re. Parkgate

Chambers, S., Hilditch, E., Place, G., and others. "Neston 1840-1940" (The Burton and South Wirral History Society 1996)

"Chester Chronicle" Various editions

Ellison, Norman. "The Wirral Peninsula" (Hale 1955)

Griffiths, Frank, the late. Author's conversations with, re. Parkgate.

Neston Parish Magazine Supplement (November 1925)

Peters, Chris, the late. (Fisherman) Author's conversations with, re. Parkgate.

Peters, Jim, the late.(Fisherman). Author's recorded conversations with, re. Parkgate.

Tudor, Joe, the late. Author's recorded conversations with, re inter-war Neston.

Chapter Seven

The Second World War

The Neston experience in the Second World War must have been similar to that of many other communities.

With the shadow of war looming ever longer throughout the late 1930s, some preparations had been made even before the outbreak of hostilities. In January 1939 Neston Urban District Council formed a Civil Defence Committee, to organise and co-ordinate air raid precautions, and, between the end of January and the end of May, volunteers were recruited for the local units of the newly-formed war emergency services, which included the Auxiliary Fire the Air Raid Precaution, and the Rescue Services.

To meet the requirements of the national black-out regulations, the hoods and mantles were removed from the street gas lamps, and the standards were painted white, to provide some help at night.

On 2nd September, the day before the declaration of war, two train loads of evacuee children arrived from Wallasey, and were soon billeted with local families. In mid-1940 a few refugee children arrived from the Channel Islands, and a very considerable number of evacuees arrived from London. Again, all were soon found temporary homes.

Soon after the beginning of the War, the Government started to build an estate of one-storey hostels on Clayhill, to house evacuee children, but, by the time the buildings were ready, in 1942, it was considered that the danger of heavy bombing had decreased to the point where they were not needed for their original purpose, and, for the remainder of the War, they were used as a naval shore establishment, "H.M.S. Mersey". To-day the Clayhill Industrial Estate occupies the site.

With the outbreak of hostilities many young men, particularly those in the Territorial Army, were called up. This exodus continued in the following years, with men and women leaving for the War as they reached the age for conscription. Some volunteered before they were called up.

Bases were established in the Area for the various emergency units. Two shop buildings on the Cross - now occupied by Balduccis Jewellers and Henry Norman, Funeral Director - were converted for use as an Auxiliary Fire Station. The old Police Station in Park Street afforded accommodation for Decontamination, Rescue, Road Repair and Casualty Service units, and the Women's Voluntary Service Manager. Air Raid Warden posts were established at various points in the Area.

Public Air Raid shelters, too, were built at a number of points, including: Brookland Road, Parkgate; Mayfield Gardens, Neston; Talbot Avenue, Badger Bait and New Street, in Little Neston; and Ness. The cellars of a number of shops and other buildings, like those in Balcony House, Parkgate and Bradley's Men's Outfitters, on the Cross (now J. A. Allister, optician), were reinforced with brick pillars or baulks of timber, and pressed into service as public shelters, mainly for the protection of those caught out shopping by a raid.

Air raid shelters were also built at the various schools. These were used by the pupils during the school day, but were made available to the general public at other times.

Many residents acquired their own shelters: either Anderson, which they sank, dug-out fashion, in their gardens, or Morrison, which were basically reinforced steel tables, with steel mesh sides, for indoor use.

A pill box was built overlooking a bend on Station Road, Parkgate, against the possibility of invasion from the Estuary. It is still there.

Again, the Committee of the Female Friendly Society suspended the Annual Walk for the duration of the War.

Two Home Guard units were formed, one at Neston and the other at Little Neston. Observation posts were established on the Parish Church Tower and on the roof of Mostyn House School by the Neston Platoon, and on the, then very high, colliery slag heaps and in a specially constructed bunker at the Old Quay House by the Little Neston Platoon.

Some fifty years later one member of the Little Neston Platoon, Robin Scott, related his experiences as a 17 to 18 year-old Home Guard, in an article written for the Burton and South Wirral History Society Bulletin. He recalled nights spent guarding the Water Tower in Lees Lane, or patrolling the roads through the local fields on the look-out for parachutists; of experiments with home-designed and made weapons; of practising signaling and fieldcraft skills; and of one particularly hair-raising occasion, when a mock night attack on a Royal Ordnance depot at Capenhurst provoked a live-ammunition response of such unbridled ferocity that the Platoon was lucky to escape without casualties. It later emerged that no one had warned the invasion-wary depot unit about the exercise.

Nestonians heard and saw much of the air attacks on Merseyside, but suffered little themselves. Frequently during the nights of 1940 and 1941 they heard the unmistakable broken rhythm of German aircraft engines passing overhead, and frequently they looked northwards to see the sky glowing red as Liverpool, Birkenhead, and Wallasey burned.

Many enemy planes caught in the box-barrage of anti-aircraft fire surrounding Merseyside jettisoned their bombs anywhere before making their escape and it was in that way that a few bombs fell on Neston, and several other places on the Dee coast.

Of the bombs dropped on Neston, the only one to cause any damage fell in the grounds of "Glenton" at the top of Bull Hill, Little Neston. It destroyed the lawn and shattered the windows of the nearby cottages.

It has often been said that the common danger and deprivations drew people throughout the country closer together during the War. It was a time of anxiety about the future, of shortages, particularly of food, clothes, and fuel, and, for many, of great personal sorrow. News of a death resulting from enemy action struck at local communities in a way that no peacetime death could. Neighbour stretched out a hand to neighbour, and to strangers, in need. It was, for example, the accepted practice for anyone caught out in the street by an air-raid to taken in at any house where they sought shelter.

All of which was as true of the Neston Area as elsewhere. Even so, there were Neston residents, as there must have been elsewhere, who could not respond to the challenge of the times. Like the man - not named here to avoid embarrassing his children - who went into Pearsons' grocery shop and begged Dick Pearson to let him have some rationed food without the immediate need for him to surrender the appropriate number of coupons. He explained that he wanted to have a meal ready for his wife, who was being discharged from the Cottage Hospital that day. His problem was that, as she had been obliged to take her ration book to the Hospital with her, he would not have the coupons in his hand until she arrived home. That being so, he promised that, if Dick would only let him have the food, he would bring the coupons to the shop before it closed for the day. Such an arrangement was strictly illegal, but Dick decided to take a chance, and let him have the food. The customer then proceeded to show his That appreciation by going straight from the shop to the Food Office, on Earle Drive, to report Dick for selling food without collecting the necessary coupons.

One evening, of unrecorded date, but probably in the late summer of 1940, the War visited a Parkgate woman in the person of a German flyer. Mrs Frances (Cissie) Bushell, who lived at the Old Watch House, had seen a German aircraft under attack by a British plane, and a number of parachutes open over the low-tide Estuary. She then watched as one man made his way across the sand and mud towards the Middle Slipway, immediately under her window, and then on, to her front door. When she opened the door to his knock, he explained, in broken English, that he was a German flyer, and offered her his pistol, as a token of surrender. With both her husband and teenage son out, and with no telephone, Cissie was uncertain about what to do. That being so, she fell back on the age-old English response to problem situations, and made her prisoner a cup of tea. She was, however, wary enough to keep him standing at the door while she made the tea and while he drank it. She then enlisted the help of a local passer-by to conduct him along the Parade to A.R.P. Warden Harold Gill's house. The German spent that night in a cell at Neston Police Station.

When asked why she had made the enemy flyer tea, as she often was, Crissie invariably replied, "Well, he looked very young - and he was somebody's son."

On 7th May 1941 two other German airmen, Lieutenant H. Dunkerbeck and Feldwebel F. Kitzing, came ashore at Parkgate, after their Heinkel had been shot down, and surrendered to a number of off-duty Home Guards. They, too, spent the night at Neston Police Station.

Both German aircraft crashed elsewhere, and, in fact, no enemy machines came down in the Neston Area.

The two planes which did crash in the Area were both British.

On 21st August 1943, the pilot of a Wellington bomber experiencing engine difficulties made a successful crash-landing on the marsh, about two hundred yards from Denhall Quay.

The other plane to crash in the Neston Area was a Mosquito fighter-bomber which flew into telegraph wires at Ness during a night exercise on 10th September 1944. The resulting explosion scattered fragments of both the machine and the two-man crew over the area now covered by the Snab Close Estate.

*32. Led by Station Officer Arthur Tillotson, the local Auxilliary Fire
Service Unit marches past the sandbag-protected Town Hall........
(Courtesy Mollie Wright)*

*33. ....Followed by the local Red Cross Unit led by Pamela Jackson.
(Courtesy Mollie Wright)*

34. *Fishermen Jim and Chris Peters in their nobby "Ethel". They saw "The Maurita" blown up on 12th November 1941.*

35. *Members of Neston and Little Neston Home Guard Platoons pose for the camera at The Old Quay House, after a combined exercise.*

36. (page 77) Neston Home Guard Platoon photographed on Sunday, 3rd December 1944, the day the Home Guard was officially stood down.

From the left:

Back: Jim Matthews; not known; Tom Tilston; Ernie Jellicoe; not known; Charles Seymour; not known; Roy Cameron; not known; not known; ? Leonard; Bill Parry; Ted Gunning.

Middle: Jack Minshell; Steve Scarrett; Walter Main; George Pearson; ? Pearce; George Fairhurst; ? Partridge; Charlie Jellicoe; Laurence Whitter; not known; Jack Parr; Harry Foote; not known.

Front: Joe Mealor; not known; George Bromelow; George Lee; Frank Hope (in civilian clothes); Ken Montgomery (commanding officer); Bill Jackson; ? Webster; Billy Cotterell; Frank Dolan; Walter Mosedale.

Mosquito was, with others, involved in ground-to-air gunnery practices on a range laid out on the marsh. These exercises, carried out by day and night, brought an unusual harvest for some locals. The prevailing, south-westerly, wind carried the parachute flares used during the night-time practices away from the target area, to come down between Ness and Burton, and exercise nights always found the fields in that area alive with figures chasing the drifting white canopies through the darkness until they finally fluttered to earth or caught on a hedge. At that time of shortages and strict clothes rationing, silk was impossible to obtain through normal channels, but, by the end of the War, more than a few Neston Area women were walking about in silk underclothes that had started life as parachutes. All of which was strictly illegal. Wartime regulations stipulated that any parachutes found by members of the public should be handed in for re-use by the R.A.F.

Of the locals who slept in their own home beds at night, it was the fishermen who saw most of the War at first hand.

In a piece written for a collection of memoirs "Wirral at War" (Countyvise 1991), the late Reg Bushell (Cissie's son), recounted something of his wartime experiences when he was a teenager working with his father, also named Reg, on their boat "Capella". Experiences that seem to have been fairly typical of those encountered by all the local fishermen. He wrote about the difficulty of navigating in the Estuary after nightfall, with no lights visible on either coast; about the experience of being inspected

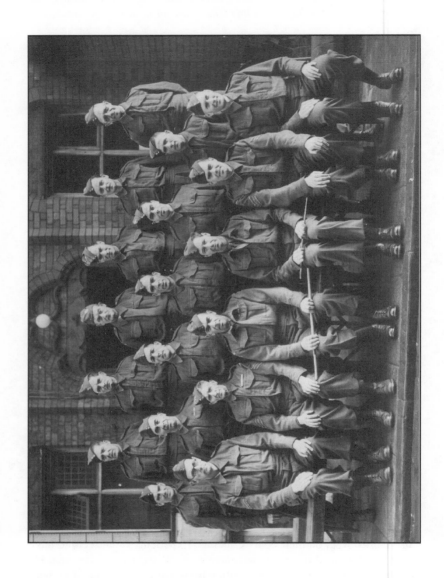

37. (opposite) The Little Neston H.G. Platoon, also photographed on 3rd December 1944.

From left:

Back: John Phillips; Frank Norman; not known; Alf Hand; Sam Smith; ? Crellin.

Centre: Jim Bartley; Bert Henderson; Alf Bailey; Charlie Lee; Bill Jones; Jim Iddon.

Front: Donald Milne; George Worthington (sergeant); Jack Henderson M.M. (lieutenant, 2nd in command); John Satterfield Hassell (captain, commanding officer); Morris Hall; John Roberts.

(Collection, Betty Smith)

by the two naval examination boats which were based at Mostyn to check on all craft entering the Liverpool Bay Area, as a precaution against spies; about the identification code flags the fisherman were supposed to fly - a regulation more honoured in the breach than the observance; and about the anti-aircraft forts that were located off Hoylake, Wallasey, and New Brighton.

These forts, looking a little like small oil rigs, were chained together in groups of four, and linked by communicating bridges.

Reg wrote of the day when he and his father were passing the New Brighton forts just as their guns opened up on some German reconnaissance planes. In a moment, the sky started to rain unexploded shells and shell splinters. Reg's father ordered him to get below, but Reg protested that, if a shell did hit them, "Capella's" wooden deck planks would afford little protection. Forced to recognise the truth of the argument, Reg senior allowed him to stay where he was and together, they watched the aircraft twisting and turning to dodge the gunfire. Happily, both "Capella" and her crew were unscathed.

There was, however, another occasion when they were not quite so lucky. And again, it was from their own side that the threat came.

Planes from Sealand and Hawarden airfields used a wreck in the mouth of the Dee Estuary, "The Nestor", for target practice, and some of the pilots would amuse themselves on their return journey by "buzzing" the fishing boats. On one occasion a fighter flew so low over "Capella" that it struck her mast, cutting it in two, and forcing the pilot to roll over and over in the sky, to rid himself of the bits of wood and steel wire his wings had collected from the rigging. The following day, an officer called at the Bushells' home, full of apologies, and with cash to pay for a new mast.

On 12th November 1941 a number of Parkgate fishermen witnessed the destruction of a coaster, by a German mine. They included the brothers Jim and Chris Peters in their boat "Ethel". Years later, Jim recounted the experience to the author.

> There were about a dozen boats working in Hilbre Swash. It was a bit foggy that day. Just after two o'clock, I looked down at my watch, and said to my brother, "It's time we went home." When I looked up again I saw a coaster coming out of the fog - it must have been about two hundred yards away. Almost as soon as I saw her, she blew up. It was a terrible sight. We all went across to the spot, but there was nothing we could do. There was nothing left except wreckage, floating on the surface. There was no sign of the crew. I believe she was the "Maurita".

"Lloyd's Register of Wartime Losses" confirm that the coaster was, indeed, the "Maurita". A vessel of 199 tons displacement, she had just left Mostyn with 240 tons of coal for Lancaster when she struck the mine. Her five-man crew were all killed.

For many during the War, there was grief to be borne with the news of a son, husband, father, or friend killed while serving with the forces or Merchant Navy, and, what was sometimes worse, notification that a loved one was missing. Occasionally, sorrow was turned to joy by the news that some long-missing relative was alive. Stanley Bailey, of Little Neston, was missing for over two years before his wife and mother heard that he was alive and held prisoner by the Japanese.

Late in 1941, Neston again learned that a local man had been awarded the V. C. George Ward Gunn, a local doctor's son, had been posthumously decorated for outstanding gallantry in North Africa. The citation read:

> On November 21st, 1941, Second-Lt Gunn was in command of a troop of four anti-tank guns, part of a battery of twelve guns attached to a rifle brigade column in Side Rezegh.
>
> Under heavy fire from 60 enemy tanks, the battery was almost destroyed, in spite of Second-Lt Gunn's efforts to re-group and encourage his men. Eventually, only two guns were left in action, and subjected to relentless fire.

38. The Cottage Hospital, 19th October 1943. Watched by Dr. George Gunn and Mrs. Gunn, Lieutenant-General E.C.A. Shreiber, General Officer Commanding Western Command, unveils a memorial plaque to 2nd Lieutenant Ward Gunn V.C., M.C., above the bed which was endowed in his honour. (Collection Flora McIlroy)

Immediately afterwards, one of these guns was blown up and the portee of the other set on fire. All the crew were wounded, except the sergeant, although the last gun itself remained undamaged.

Second-Lt. Gunn ran to the emplacement through intense fire and put the gun into action on the burning portee, the sergeant acting as loader. Regardless of the concentrated enemy fire, Second-Lt. Gunn's shooting was so accurate at a distance of 800 yards that at least two enemy tanks were hit and set on fire and three others were badly damaged.

At any moment the fire might have reached the ammunition with which the portee was loaded, but the two men fought on until Second-Lt. Gunn fell dead, the victim of a stray bullet which shattered his forehead.

Twice in 1945 Nestonians danced on the Cross: once following the German surrender in May 1945, and again in August, when the Japanese capitulated.

Of those who marched away to war, 61 failed to return.

SOURCES NOT MENTIONED IN THE TEXT

Bushell, Ina. Author's interview with re. Cissie Bushell's encounter with the German flyer.

Author's own memories.

Cyril Jones (of Ness). Author's interview with re the crashed Mosquito

"Lloyds' Second World War Losses. Volume 1 British, Allied, and Neutral Vessels Sunk or Destroyed by War Causes." (Lloyds of London Press 1989)

Information concerning German airmen captured at Parkgate in May 1941 supplied by Steven Parsons of the Aircraft Museum at Hooton, and passed on to the Author by E. Hilditch

Neston Urban District Council Records. (Access to the files arranged by Anne Tudor, Information Officer, Neston Town Hall.)

Scarrett, Steve. Former Neston Home Guard. Author's interview with.

Tudor, Joe, the late. Former Little Neston Home Guard. Author's interview with.

Chapter Eight

A Pleasant Place to Live

The thirty years, or so, between the end of the Second World War and the merging of Neston and Ellesmere Port local authorities saw a rapid expansion of the Neston Area.

Beginning with the Rose Gardens Estate at Little Neston in 1947, council and private housing was erected at an average rate of 180 dwellings a year in the 1950s and 1960s, to meet the needs of a swelling population. It was an expansion that covered the fields that had separated Neston, Parkgate, Little Neston and Ness, and blurred the separate identities of those settlements.

"An Outline Plan for Neston Urban District," published by Neston Urban District Council in 1946, visualised the future of Parkgate as a "quiet resort", based on the construction of a marine lake, but the proposal has remained nothing more than an idea.

The end of the War brought a need to find work for the returning demobilised men and women.

When the evacuee hostels on Clayhill were vacated by the Navy, in 1945, many of them were commandeered by squatters as housing accommodation. In 1948 the Estate was transferred from Government jurisdiction to that of Neston Council, which allowed the continued use of the buildings for housing until sufficient council houses were available. As the tenants moved to housing on the new estates, small industrial concerns were granted the tenancy of some of the former hostel buildings.

In 1949 The Council approved a plan for the Estate to be developed as a site for light industries, and, in the 1960s, when it was considered that some capital could be diverted from housing, the hostel buildings were gradually demolished, the estate roads were improved, and new factory units were built and rented to various small industrial concerns.

39. Looking up the High Street from Bridge Street in the late 1950s. The building projecting out into the road on the left was demolished in the 1960s, and the shop on the extreme right has been converted and incorporated into an office development. The bank is now an Asian restaurant. (Collection Ian Boumphrey)

By the beginning of the seventies some of the Clayhill units were occupied by a variety of enterprises, employing about a hundred workers between them. They included two light engineering companies, a bakery, a monumental works, and a company engaged in the manufacture of lampshades.

It was very largely due to the Council's efforts to attract employment to the Neston Area that, in 1949, the Morgan Crucible Company of Battersea established a factory on a site to the immediate north of Liverpool Road. Manufacturers of such products as refractory cements, insulating firebricks, and various specialised items for the same industrial field, the Company was able to recruit some five hundred workers from the Area

Many people employed in the factories and offices of Merseyside found Neston a pleasant place in which to live. Surrounded on three sides by

40. Neston Cross c1960. (Courtesy Guyse Williams)

41. 1955. Loading firebricks at Morgan Refractories factory.
(Courtesy Messrs Morganite Thermal Ceramics)

Green Belt Areas - for what they are worth - and overlooking the open spaces of the Dee Estuary, it is outside the Merseyside Conurbation and yet conveniently situated for easy travel by car or public transport.

A link with pre-war days was lost when Parkgate Baths closed in the early 1950s. By that time so few tides reached Parkgate that the owners could no longer change the water at frequent intervals. The empty pool areas were used as refuse dumps until they were full, and the site was converted to its present use as a country park picnic area in the 1970s.

The census returns made between 1951 and 1971 revealed that about 55% of the gainfully-occupied population as travelling daily to places outside the Area. Ministry of Labour statistics showed that, although some of the remaining 45% of workers were employed in local industries, the majority were employed in service occupations associated with the residential character of the district, such as shop work, and the various occupations connected with the building trade.

While it was basically the same pattern that had been established by the opening of the Hooton-Parkgate Railway in 1866, the town was no longer dependent on the Railway to carry its commuters and goods. In the period following the War railways in general had begun to lose traffic to the resurgent and expanding road transport industry, and the 1950s, with their spectacular increase in car ownership, saw large numbers of passengers deserting the railways for the roads. Of course, the Hooton-West Kirby line was not immune from these forces. Business declined to the point where it was no longer economic to maintain passenger services, and, on 15th September 1956, the last passenger train ran from West-Kirby to Hooton. The line remained open for the carriage of a shrinking volume of goods until 1962, when it was finally closed. In 1966 the track was raised, and in 1966 both Neston and Parkgate stations were dismantled. The Seacombe line survived largely on the iron-ore traffic which was carried from Bidston Dock to Shotton.

The late 1950s brought the first of a series of long-overdue school-building projects to the Area.

It was a scheme to meet Neston Urban District's need for a secondary school. A need that had originally been recognised in the early 1930s. Cheshire County Council had even bought a field off Mellock Lane as a site for the building, but procrastination had delayed the project, and the outbreak of war had killed it off.

In the post-war period it soon became obvious that the need for a secondary school had become urgent. The existing elementary schools were struggling with the near-impossible duty of providing an all-age education for a rapidly-expanding child population, a task that was made even more onerous after 1948, when the leaving age was raised to fifteen. A few scholarship pupils gained places at grammar schools, but the vast majority received their teenage education at the same schools where they had enrolled as infants. Schools which were not equipped or staffed to provide an adequate secondary education.

Even so, Neston was just one of a number of places that lacked a county secondary school, and, as such, it had to wait its turn.

Work finally started in the mid-1950s, on a site off Raby Park Road.

The new, mixed-sex, school admitted its first pupils, with its buildings still unfinished, on 6th January 1958. Initially, there were twelve members of staff and two hundred and forty pupils. Within a year the number of pupils had risen to three hundred and sixty.

Although it was known as "Neston Secondary Modern School", with a number of specialist teachers on the staff and teaching areas provided for

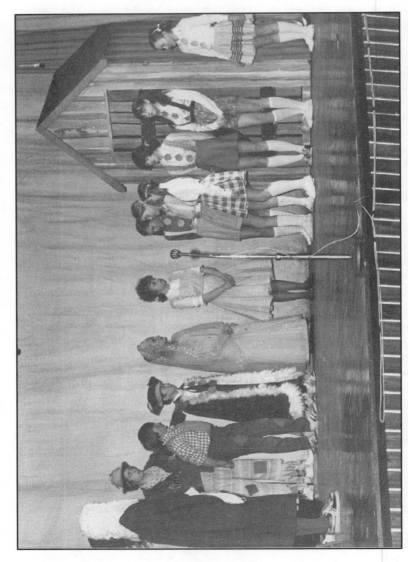

42. 1975. Scene from Neston Comprehensive (now 'High') School's production of "The Wizard of Oz".
(Courtesy Ada Knox)

technical subjects, such as metalwork, woodwork, technical drawing, and needlework, it was, in fact, officially classified as a secondary modern/secondary technical school.

The opening of the new school provoked a direct-action protest by some parents. They were among those who had judged the quality of education offered at the old, all-age, schools to be inadequate, and had managed gain admission for their children to one of the new Pensby Secondary Modern schools - then still in Cheshire - before the Neston school was available. They were very satisfied with Pensby, and reacted angrily to the County's instructions that they should transfer their children to Neston. When the head teachers at Pensby, under instruction from County Hall, turned the Neston pupils away, the parents responded by keeping their boys and girls at home. It was about a month before they finally agreed to send their children to Neston.

In September 1972 the school became comprehensive. The number of pupils rose from the five hundred and fifty attending the Secondary Modern School to nearly fifteen hundred in five years. They were taught by eighty, or so, teachers, and the School functioned with the assistance of some sixty ancillary staff, such as cooks, cleaners, office staff, and lab technicians. Known when it first accepted an unselected pupil entry as "Neston County Comprehensive School", it was later re-named "Neston County High School."

During the fifteen years, or so, which followed the opening of the Secondary School, most of the primary schools in the Area moved to new buildings, or were replaced by new schools, the old buildings having been declared inadequate or below standard. The two exceptions were the former Council School, which had passed into County control in 1948 as "Neston Primary School", and Liverpool Road.

Junior pupils from Liverpool Road were transferred to a new school on Raby Park Road - "Raby Park School" - in 1961, but Liverpool Road survived as an infants' school until 1992.

The Parkgate Infants' School closed in 1968, and its pupils transferred to a new "Parkgate County Primary School".

Ness Holt School closed after its pupils had been transferred, in stages, to two new schools off Woodfall Lane: the juniors in 1967 and the infants in 1969.

43. March 1974. The members of the last Neston Urban District Council, and their principal officers, photographed in Neston Town Hall Council Chamber. (Councillor unless otherwise stated).

From left: Denis O'Brien; Richard Thomas; Brian Jenkins (Treasurer); Fred Barker; Harold Brooks; Reg Chrimes; Peter Robson; Mrs. Pauline Hatton (Chairman's Lady); Len Mcbradley; Gordon Hatton (Chairman of Council); Norman Angel; Gerald Carr (Public Health Inspector); Bill Howe; Tim Prior; John Herbert; Cyril Price (Chief Executive); Sid Beech (Housing Officer); William Newton; Sid Pequignot; Peter Jones; Tom Aldridge (Engineer and Surveyor).

(Courtesy Ada Knox)

Similarly, St. Winifride's School made a two-phase move from the old Burton Road building to a new building on Mellock Lane in 1967 and 1974.

On 16th May 1958, the Urban District Council re-established Neston Market as an indoor market at the Institute (now the Civic Hall). Disappointingly for the romantically-minded, perhaps, it did not, as heir of the Mostyns, invoke the 1728 Charter, but used, instead, the powers vested in it by the various modern local government acts.

The Market was transferred to the basement at the Town Hall in September 1965. There it continued as an indoor market until 1967, when it was extended to include an outdoor area.

In April 1974 Neston Urban District Council was merged with the Borough of Ellesmere Port in a district authority, which is now known as The Borough of Ellesmere Port and Neston. Although the merger was almost certainly disliked by the majority of Nestonians, it was widely accepted as the price that had to be paid to escape from the danger of being absorbed into the new, synthetic, county of Merseyside.

SOURCES NOT MENTIONED IN THE TEXT

"Birkenhead News". Various editions.

Chrimes, Councillor Reg, Author's recorded conversation with re. Neston Urban District Council.

Hird, Bob (First Headteacher Neston Secondary and Neston Comprehensive Schools), Author's recorded conversation with

Railway History Group "The Hooton to West Kirby Branch Line and The Wirral Way." (Metropolitan Borough of Wirral, 1982)

Ministry of Labour. "Returns for the Neston Office" (1964)

Morgan Refractories Ltd. "How Came Neston." (1949)

Neston Urban District Council Records. (Access to the files arranged by Anne Tudor, Information Officer, Neston Town Hall.)

Appendix A

Fishermen of Parkgate

Today it is difficult to visualise Parkgate as a busy fishing haven. Yet, only sixty years ago some thirty full-time fishermen worked from the village. To those can be added as many again who combined part-time fishing with some other part-time job, such as gardening, chauffeuring, or smallholding.

Not all the local fishermen lived at Parkgate. Most did, but some lived at Neston or Little Neston. Even so, almost all used Parkgate as their working base, and Parkgate Station was very much the fishermen's station. That being the case, the fishermen living in the Neston Area may be conveniently and fairly grouped as "Parkgate fishermen". All wore the distinctive navy-blue fishermen's guernsey (locally pronounced "gansey").

After the failure of the herring fisheries, in the 1820s, fishing fell to the level of a marginal economic activity. The 1841 Census Return revealed that there were only thirteen fishermen living at Parkgate, with a few others living in other parts of the Neston Area. The Parkgate Census Returns for 1851 and 1861 listed twelve and sixteen fishermen respectively.

The small number of fishermen in the first two-thirds of the nineteenth century was directly related to the small market that was available to them. There was no shortage of fish. Even after the herrings had failed, there plenty of other types of fish to be caught. The problem was one of transport. Herrings could be cured, by salting or smoking, packed in barrels, and then, if necessary, carried long distances to inland markets by the very slow means of transport then available. There was, however, no method of preserving the other types of fish caught in the Dee Estuary and Liverpool Bay. Flatfish, like flukes (flounders), plaice, and skate, and shellfish, particularly shrimps, mussels, and cockles, had to be sold as quickly as possible after being landed, otherwise they would have deteriorated to the point where they would have become inedible. This meant that the market available to the Parkgate fishermen before the coming of the railway to the village was a very local one, probably comprising Wirral, Chester, and central Liverpool.

The advent of the Hooton to Parkgate Railway, in 1866, changed the situation completely. The new Railway became a powerful stimulus to fishing activity at Parkgate. In particular, it opened a great market for cockles and mussels in the industrial cities and towns of South Lancashire and Yorkshire.

Shrimps were mostly caught in the summer months, although there was often a long overlap with the beginning of the cockle/mussel season.

The Railway also brought a market to Parkgate, in the persons of crowds of week-end day-trippers set on completing their outings to the seaside by treating themselves to the, then new, indulgence of a shrimp tea, and/or by taking a bag of shrimps, or a jar of pickled cockles or mussels home with them. Several cafes were opened, and two or three fisherfolk whose front doors gave on to the Parade set up sales tables, to meet these twin demands (Illustration 46)

Those tables were very effective outlets. Former Parkgate fishermen Hughie Higgins remembers how his family sold everything they caught - wet fish, shrimps, and cockles - over their table.

The fish sold from the tables could not have been more fresh. On one occasion, in the nineteen-forties, a customer objected that a fluke that Hughie had placed on the scale pan for her was not fresh. Hughie replied that he personally had landed it from the boat within the hour.

"But it can't be fresh - it's covered in slime, " she persisted.

As if on cue, the fish jumped off the scales, and on to the table.

Hughie picked it up, and replaced it on the scales.

"Is that fresh enough for you?" he enquired politely.

He then went on to explain that a coating of slime was a sure indication that a fish was still alive.

Other fishermen negotiated agreements with cafes, shops, and hotels.

Following the coming of the Railway, the numbers of fishermen living in Parkgate rose from the sixteen in 1861, already mentioned, to twenty-five in 1871, with a further seventeen living in Neston. By 1891 it had risen to forty-six at Parkgate, and twenty-one in other parts of the Neston Area.

Until the early 1920s all fishing boats on the Dee Estuary worked under sail.

For many years the traditional Parkgate fishing boat was the yawl. Known locally as a "jigger boat", it was a two-masted, shallow-draught vessel that was particularly well-suited to local conditions.

About 1900, however, a new type of fishing boat appeared in the Dee Estuary. Technically described as a Morecambe Bay Prawner, to the fishermen it was never anything else but a "nobby".

Single-masted vessels, which ranged in length from twenty to thirty-five feet, nobbies were specially designed for work in the shallow coastal waters of the north-west coast. Their shallow draught enabled them to sail over sandbanks, where shrimps and flatfish feed, and their great sail area allowed them to draw a heavy beam trawl over the bottom.

The new boats proved so popular with the local fishermen that, over the course of the following thirty years the nobby completely displaced the jigger boat as the standard Dee fishing boat.

Another type of craft, used for the mundane task of cockle and mussel gathering, was the large rowing boat known locally as a "punt". With these boats the fishermen could drift down river on the ebb-tide to sandbanks and mudflats near the mouth of the Estuary, spend the day raking for shellfish, and return to Parkgate on the next incoming tide. Punts were also used as tenders to carry the men and their catches between the big boats, moored out in the channel and the shore.

Some fishermen did not own a boat, and earned a living by hand netting. This involved pushing a hand shrimping net at the edge of the tide, or in the flooded gutters left behind at low tide, or setting stake nets on the sandbanks at low tide, for flukes and grey mullet. (Illustration 47)

Parkgate fishing folk were an independent people, who took a fierce pride in being their own masters.

At the same time, there was a strong community spirit. One of the ways in which this spirit manifested itself was in the nicknames used openly, and cheerfully acknowledged by the fishermen. They included "Dick Dophy" (Joe Smith); "Billy Why-Why" (William Mealor); "Bad Luck" (William Campion) Ragger (Jim Campion), and "Spurna" (John Smith).

"Spurna" seems to have been a remarkable character, well-liked and respected by everyone who knew him. A huge man and, in his youth, a notable local athlete, he was always ready to lend the benefit of his uncanny strength to anyone whose boat needed moving.

44. Fishermen cleaning and bagging mussels on the Middle Slip c1930. During the inter-war years some twenty to thirty bags of shellfish were dispatched from Parkgate Station every week to some of the industrial towns of south Lancashire and Yorkshire. (Collection Ina Bushell)

45. 1935. Jack (Caggy) Mealor's nobby "Sunbeam" lying aground off the sea wall. The building on the right was the Parkgate Convalescent Home. It was demolished in the 1950s, and part of Dee Court now stands on the site. (Collection Ina Bushell)

46. Selling fish from the doorways of fishermen's cottages on The Parade, Parkgate c1930. (From a painting by Eleanor Whinnery. Collection Williamson Art Gallery)

The community spirit was always particularly evident in times of trouble. For Parkgate fishing families, as for fishing folk everywhere, tragedy and death were never far away, and it was in moments of crisis that neighbour drew close to neighbour.

There was, for example, the occasion when the boats were caught out by a sudden storm on 19th December 1919. They struggled back through the darkness and turmoil to their moorings, located, for the state of the tide as it then was, a little below the village, with great difficulty.

On the following morning word went round that George (Slen) Mellor, who had been working his jigger boat, "Joseph and Mary" single-handed, had failed to return to his Neston home. A search party of fishermen found "Joseph and Mary" secured to her mooring chain, and Slen's body lying on the sandbank beside it. He had, apparently, fallen into the sea and drowned while he was trying to scramble from his boat and into the punt he used as a tender.

97

47. A handnet fisherman sets out a line of stake nets.
(Courtesy Harry Jones)

Fate dealt the Mellor Family another blow just a year, or so, later, when Slen's seventeen-year-old nephew, his brother's son, also named George, was drowned. He had been working on his father's boat, fishing off Mostyn, when the boom swung and knocked him overboard. Immediately, his sea boots filled with water, and dragged him down.

His father called to Fred and Bill Higgins, who were trawling nearby in their nobby "Kingfisher", to help look for the boy. They hauled in their net, preparatory to joining the search, only to find young Mellor's body in it.

But there were happy times, too. The great annual event in the village calendar before the First World War was the Parkgate Fishermen's Regatta, held in June or July, according to the suitability of the tides.

For weeks before the event all the talk was of the races and the competitors. From Heswall, Thurstaston, and all the other anchorages on the Estuary, fishermen called at Parkgate to hand in their entries.

On the day itself the buildings along the Parade were festooned with flags and bunting, and a band was hired for the occasion.

The first race to be started was always that for nobbies, and the second was for jigger boats.

Both the nobby and jigger boat races were held over a triangular course that ran from Parkgate down to Heswall, and across the Estuary to Mostyn and back to Parkgate, a distance of some fifteen miles. It was a course that required competitors to work both with and against the wind and the tide.

While these larger boats were battling it out in the distance, the spectators on the Parade were able to watch the small sailing boat and rowing boat races.

After the finish of each of the two main races the winning boat sailed a lap of honour, streaming the victor's pennant on a short course that ran parallel to the Parade, while the band, seated on the Donkey Stand, played the melody of a song that included some mention of the winning boat's name. For example, when Dick Peters won the nobby race in his boat "Onward", the band played "Onward Christian Soldiers."

Some names must have taxed the musicians' ingenuity, but it is said that none of the bandmasters ever failed to think of an appropriate musical tribute.

Prizes were always cash.

48. Nobbies racing at a Parkgate Fisherman's Regatta. On the left Maurice Evans's "Amy"; on the right Fred Higgins "Kingfisher".

49. George Henry (Swad) Jones shrimping with his horse 'Sandy' and trap. (Collection Harry Jones)

50. Swad transfers his catch from his net to a bucket. (Collection Harry Jones)

After the competitors had eaten the very substantial high tea that was provided, the festivities came to an end with children's games and dancing on the Green, an area behind the Parade houses that has since disappeared under housing development.

The last successful regatta was held in 1914 and, although attempts to revive the Event were made in 1920 and 1921 they were both marred by unfavourable weather. It was, however the advent of the marine engine on the Estuary which brought an end to the Regatta. Increasingly, in the 1920s, fishermen fitted engines, dismantled their boats' rigging, and reduced the height of their masts by half. To re-rig the boats for one race every year would have been prohibitively time-consuming and costly.

In the later 1930s working out of Parkgate became increasingly difficult. That being so, the fishermen took to mooring their boats at Heswall or Thurstaston and commuting to these anchorages in vans. After the Second World War conditions became so difficult that no young men entered the trade.

In addition to the distinction of being the last fisherman to work from a base in the Neston Area, George Henry (Swad) Jones, was possibly the only one ever to trawl for shrimps with a horse and trap on the Dee Estuary.

Working from Quayside, Little Neston, Swad trawled the water-filled gutters left by the retreating tide with his pony 'Sandy', and a small trap for some twenty years in the 1940s and 50s. (See illustrations 49 and 50)

The story is told of an occasion when Swad was out shrimping with an assistant "Monk" Jones. After several hours, the sight of the incoming tide had signalled that it was time to return to the shore. They set off for Quayside, with the pony pulling the loaded trap, but, before they had got very far, Sandy fell into a patch of quicksand. In a moment he sank up to his withers (i.e. front shoulders). Swad and Monk uncoupled the trap, and then pulled and pushed the pony in a desperate attempt to extricate him before he was overwhelmed by the tide. For his part, Sandy heaved and thrashed to the very limited extent that he was able to do. All to no avail. Try as they might, the pony was too deeply trapped for them to get him out. With the first tongues of water licking at the animal's neck, Swad had to face the fact that they would have to leave him to his fate. Heavy-hearted, the men picked up the shafts of the trap, and, pulling it between them, resumed their homewards trek. They trudged on over the sands, with tears streaming down Swad's cheeks. Unwilling to see the pony die, Swad stared resolutely ahead, but, after half a mile or so, Monk turned and looked back.

"Look here!" he exclaimed, his voice suddenly joyful.

Swad turned.

There was Sandy, two hundred yards behind them, trotting briskly to catch up.

SOURCES NOT MENTIONED IN THE TEXT

Author's own knowledge and observation of Neston and Parkgate since 1940.

Author's own experiences as a boy accompanying Jim and Chris Peters on fishing trips during the school holidays.

Higgins, Hughie (former Parkgate fisherman) Author's conversations with.

Locket, Alan "North Western Sail" (Countryside Publications) 1978

Merseyside Railway Group "The Hooton to West Kirby Branch Line" (Metropolitan Borough of Wirral) 1982

Parkgate Fishermen's Regatta 1914 Programme

Peters, Chris, the late (former Parkgate fisherman) author's conversations with.

Peters, Chris "List of Parkgate Fishermen with Their Boats" (Unpublished) 1986

Peters, Jim, the late (former Parkgate fisherman) author's recorded conversation with.

Appendix B

The Mines

Even in its present tumbledown state, the old mine quay, close to the "Harp" inn is an impressive relic of an important and fascinating aspect of Neston history (illustration 51).

Built in the middle of the eighteenth century to serve the Denhall Colliery at a time when coastwise shipping offered the only economical means of carrying bulk goods about the country, the Quay was also a suitable place from which to export coal to overseas destinations.

In the Dee Estuary context of small ships only, the loading berth in front of the Quay must have been very deep in its working days. As recently as the late 1940s, after nearly a century of silting, there was still enough water left to make a deep swimming hole when the tide was out.

Mining activity in the Area was based an outlier of the North Wales coalfield that occupies a small area to the south of Neston.

The existence of evidence revealing that coal was mined in the Area in Roman times has already been mentioned in Chapter One. That being the case, it seems probable that small-scale, open-cast and shallow "drift", mining was carried on in the centuries that followed, a supposition that finds some support from the occasional entry of "miner" in Neston Parish Registers after 1727, when incumbents started to note the occupations of those whose names they recorded.

The Stanley Family of Hooton and Denna Hall opened the first large-scale colliery in 1757, importing miners from Lancashire, Staffordshire, and North Wales to work it.

The Pithead and Quay were located on the Stanley's land, just inside the Ness-Denhall township boundary (see Map 6), but, after the rights had been leased from the Cottingham Family, joint Lords of the Manor of Little Neston, some of the workings passed under the boundary and into the township of Little Neston.

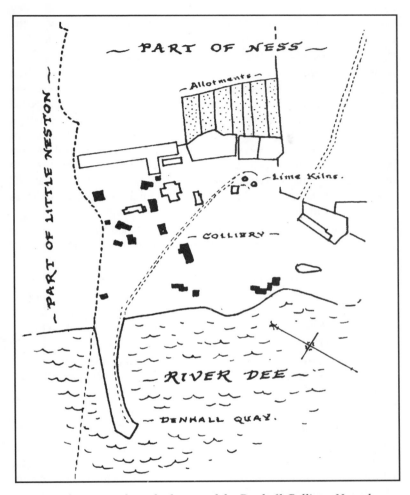

Map 6. Map to show the layout of the Denhall Colliery. Note the railway line from the Quay, and the lime kiln. It seems that the coal sloops carried limestone as a return cargo and as ballast. When the limestone was reduced to lime in the kiln it would have been sold to farmers for spreading on their fields. (Based on the 1846 Tithe Map)

105

For many years this Ness Mine possessed a feature of special interest: the coal was transported from the coal face to the bottom of the shaft along two underground canals. Mortimer, in his book "The History of the Hundred of Wirral", stated that there were two canals, one at a depth of sixty yards, and one at ninety-four yards below the surface.

Almost certainly, the barges used were similar to the so-called "starvationers" that were being built at that time for the canals in the Worsley mines. Long, narrow, shallow, and flat-bottomed, with exposed ribs that earned them their peculiar nick-name, the boats in the Denhall pit carried four baskets containing four hundredweights each - a sort of eighteenth century container system. Four or five boats were roped together in a train, and then propelled along the canals by miners who lay with their backs on planks placed across the boats' gunwales, and then "walked" along the roof, taking the barges with them. As might be expected, progress was slow - Mortimer mentioned a speed of a mile an hour.

Early in the nineteenth century the Stanleys seemed to have had some doubts about the mine because an advertisement appeared in "The Courant" of 29th August 1812,

> To let for any term not exceeding 30 years. Ness Colliery, close to the River Dee, where coals are shipped off an extensive and convenient quay for Ireland, North and South Wales, and then Isle of Man. Together with a farm of about 90 stature acres etc., adjoining the works etc.
>
> The coal consists of three veins of 6, 5, and 7 feet respectively, as well of one of two feet. Under the last there is a seam of excellent fire clay etc., etc.
>
> For further particulars, application should be made to Mr. Ashurst of Puddington.

On one occasion, at least, Ness/Denhall coal was shipped to a much further destination than those mentioned in the advertisement. An entry in the Glegg Account Book for 1764 mentions a ship which sailed from the Mine Quay with a part-cargo for Philadelphia.

There seems to have been a shortage of suitable applicants to lease the Mine because the Stanleys carried on managing it themselves for the next forty years or so.

In 1819 the Stanleys' lease on the part of the coal seams which ran under Cottinghams' Little Neston land expired, and Thomas Cottingham decided to work his own deposits himself.

Neston & Parkgate Remembered

The two landlords were mining different parts of the same seam.

In 1821, and again in 1822, Thomas Cottingham sued Sir Thomas Stanley for trespass, alleging that some of his men had worked in the Little Neston tunnels. On both occasions the Court found in favour of Cottingham, and Stanley was fined £200 for the first trespass, and £2,000 for the second, which had involved Cottingham in some loss of production.

The underground canals were pumped out during the 1820s, and were replaced by a railway system for "tubs", drawn by pit ponies.

In Little Neston, the Cottinghams worked their seams from pits on both sides of Colliery Lane (now Marshlands Road).

At both collieries profitability was only maintained with difficulty. Both were open at the time of the 1841 Census, but, although the 1846 Tithe Map and Apportionment of Ness marks the pithead workings of the Denhall mine and records Charles Stanley as the owner, the 1849 Tithe Map for Little Neston shows no working pits in that township.

The 1841 Census recorded 94 colliers as living in the Parish of Neston.

The 1851 Census recorded 120 workers as employed in the Ness/Denhall Colliery. Despite the Mines Act of 1842, which had prohibited the employment of anyone under 10, the total included two nine-year-old boys.

The Census made no reference to any Little Neston pit.

On the night of the Census a coal sloop, "The Mary", was recorded as lying off the colliery. The Master was 28-year-old William Griffiths, and the Mate was Thomas Davies, aged 20.

In 1855 the Stanleys finally abandoned the enterprise. The mine was closed, and its equipment sold. Giving evidence to a Parliamentary Inquiry that was considering the re-opening of the workings in 1869, Thomas Cottingham, a mining engineer whose father had owned the Little Neston Pit, stated,

> The reasons why Ness Colliery was given up was, I believe, it was presumed to be exhausted as regards the 2 feet, the 7 feet and the 5 feet (seams).

He also added that he thought the costs of the 1822 lawsuit had eventually proved too heavy a burden for the Stanleys.

In 1859 Lord Mostyn's agent commissioned a survey to assess the probable profitability of a mine on Mostyn's residual Parkgate lands. Although the Report was generally encouraging, Lord Mostyn did not pursue the matter.

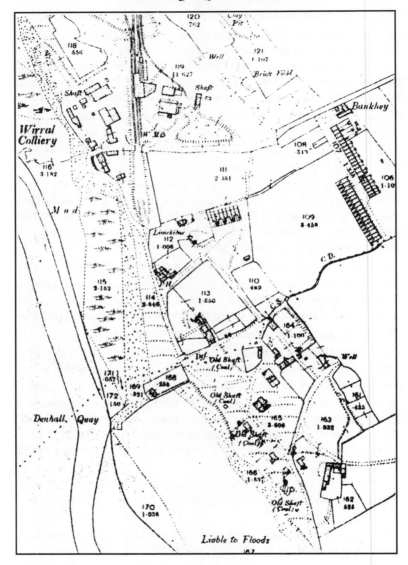

Map 7. The 1899 Ordnance Survey Map shows the location of Little Neston Colliery. (Scale Denhall Quay to Little Neston Colliery= 1/2 mile)

In 1874 Charles Mott of Birkenhead took out a forty-year lease on the mineral rights of some 1,000 acres from the trustees of the Earl of Shrewsbury. A few months later, The Neston Colliery Company, an enterprise formed for the purpose, bought out Mott's rights and, on 5th April 1875, a party of Company directors and their ladies performed the ceremony of cutting the first sod for a new shaft on the site of one of the old Little Neston workings.(See Map 7)

To secure a means of bulk transport for the coal, a railway spur was built from a point at Moorside on the Hooton-Parkgate line.

By the time the new pit was opened, all of the experienced colliers who had worked the old mines were dead, or were too old to work, or had settled on some other type of employment. The 1871 Census had listed only five men as miners living in the Neston Area. Even so, there was no shortage of skilled labour. News of the new pit soon spread and generated a rapid influx of colliers from other mining districts. These skilled men were joined by a number of, presumably inexperienced, Nestonians. Of the 147 colliery workers recorded in the 1881 Census as living in the Area, 64 had been born in Wales; 30 in Lancashire; 33 in Neston Parish; and the remainder from a variety of places.

Between 1875 and 1880, the Company built two rows of terraced cottages for miners close to the Pit, on what became known as New Street. These cottages could, however, accommodate, only a part of the workforce. Most mineworkers lived in houses scattered throughout the Neston Area.

Working conditions in the Mine were unpleasant. Almost inevitably in a pit where the tunnels ran, at their furthest extent, some two miles out under an Estuary, the workings were subject to heavy water seepage, and continuous pumping was necessary to prevent flooding. The small additional allowance paid to those who were obliged to work crouching in icy water can hardly have compensated for the misery involved.

Another unpleasant feature of the Mine was the vermin that infested the workings. Mice and cockroaches were the miners' ever-present companions. One of the first lessons every new man learnt was to carry his sandwiches in a tin box; if he carried them in a cloth or wrapped in paper, they would be eaten before his break arrived.

The presence of these pests seems to have been connected with the use of pit ponies in the Mine. The warmth of the underground stables and the food and water provided for the animals may have fostered the conditions that allowed the vermin to thrive. Certain it is that when the number of ponies was much reduced after the introduction of additional machinery during the First World War, there was a noticeable fall in the vermin level.

The ponies were used in the small side workings which were not reached by the continuous, moving rope of the main roadway. The ponies drew the small wagons, known as "boxes" ("tubs" in many other mines), each containing half a ton of coal, to a point where they could be attached to the continuous cable.

The number of boxes pulled by a pony was usually five. Independently of each other, and on different occasions, former miners the late Joe Peters and the late Joe Tudor told the Author that one pony, Khaki, actually appeared to be able to count. The ponies had to wait in harness while their trains were assembled, and, as each box was added to the train the coupling would clank. If an attempt was made to add an extra box to Khaki's train - if there was more than the right number of clanks - he would refuse to budge, and nothing would induce him to move until the offending box had been taken off.

Although no large-scale disaster seems to have occurred at the Little Neston Pit, it was, like most mines, a dangerous place. Common mishaps included injuries caused when fragments invaded eyes, often during shot-firing; when men were accidentally struck with picks wielded by workmates; and when fingers were caught between boxes and rails. Over the years, a number of men were killed in rock falls, and there was the ever-present threat posed by pockets of methane gas.

Accidents, a number of them fatal also occurred on the surface. One victim of a surface accident was 17-year-old Richard Roberts was killed on 6th March 1917, when he slipped under a wagon in the sidings.

Almost incredibly, the Company made no provision for the care and treatment of injured men. There was no first-aid room and no first-aid staff. Nothing. "Not even a bandage," emphasised former miner George Tilley.

At the inquest on Fred Abel, the last man to be killed in the Pit, Dr. Gunn stated that only recently a miner had been brought in to the Cottage Hospital with some of his fingers knocked off. "There was no dressing, except his own scarf, on the wound."

The Coroner was evidently not interested, because he abruptly changed the direction of his questioning.

51. Remains of the old mine quay at Denhall. (Courtesy E.T.W. Dennis & Sons Ltd.)

52. Former miners' cottages in New Street, Little Neston, photographed in 1960, but still looking much as they must have done when they were built by the Neston Mining Company in 1875. Miners lived in all parts of the area, but the Management obviously thought that it would be in the Company's interests to have some men living close to the pithead. The appearance of the rows has since been much altered by individual owners who have changed the facades of their own houses to suit their personal tastes.

53. 12th March 1927. The last shift. From left: Arthur Jones; Dave Parry; Joe Burkey; Joe Millington; Bill Williams; Richie Williams; John M. Williams; Jack Campion; Henry Williams and Jim Jones. (Collection Ian Boumphrey)

And there was no provision for taking seriously-injured men to the nearest hospital, which until 1920, when the Cottage Hospital was opened (See Appendix E), was Clatterbridge. The almost invariable practice in such cases was for a workmate to help the casualty home - losing an hour or two's wages in the process. Once at home, the injured man would decide whether he could afford the expense of sending for a doctor, or not.

Like most workpeople at the time, the Little Neston mineworkers received no pay when they were absent from work, sick or otherwise. Many provided against the possibility of sickness and, indeed, death, by joining a friendly society, which would pay out sickness and death benefits when needed. More often than not, they chose the local branch of the Shepherds' Club. Even so, such payments could not, of course, compensate for the lack of adequate first-aid treatment at the Pithead, or for the lack of suitable ambulance provision.

Frederick Abel was working in the Pit on 22nd January 1926, when his 24-year-old son, also named Frederick, was struck by a falling rock just a few yards away from him. Father Fred picked up his son and carried him to the bottom of the shaft. Once at the surface, he placed young Fred on his shoulder, and ran all the way to the Cottage Hospital on Little Neston Green, a distance of a mile, and almost every yard of it uphill. At the Hospital, Dr. Gunn pronounced young Fred to be dead.

It was almost certainly a consciousness of their vulnerability that rendered the miners a generally superstitious lot. Presumably afraid of instant divine retribution, men who blasphemed freely on the surface took care to bridle their tongues underground. Swearing was all but unknown in the workings. Similarly, when Bill Jones was killed by a fall, on 2nd June 1924, his cap - this was long before the days of miners' helmets - lay on the underground roadway for hours before some unrecorded hero finally picked it up. The fear being that he who picked it up would also pick up Bill's luck.

The Mine was finally closed because it could not be operated economically. On several occasions the company that worked it went into voluntary liquidation, to be replaced by another which, in turn, folded. Thus, "Neston Colliery Ltd." was succeeded by "Wirral Colliery Ltd." which, in its turn, was replaced by "Wirral Colliery (1915) Ltd." The problem was not caused by high operating costs. Indeed, operating costs appear to have been below average: at no point was the Mine deeper than three hundred feet; the seams were fairly thick, and, therefore, easy to work; and by selling much of the coal at the pithead to the railways, transport costs could be reduced to a minimum. The main difficulty was that of selling the steam coal, the bulk of the output, at a price which covered the cost of its production. The household coal could be sold on the Wirral Peninsula at a profit, but the force of competition from other collieries ensured that the large consumers, to whom steam coal might be sold, could buy the coal at a price that frequently fell below the cost of production.

In 1916, to further the First World War effort , the Mine, together with mines elsewhere, was taken into public ownership. As maximum output was needed, irrespective of cost, operations were maintained with the help of government subsidies.

In 1921 the Mine was returned to the ownership of Wirral Colliery (1915) Ltd. Almost at once the Company began to experience the same difficulties which had dogged its predecessors before the War, and by August 1922 the 330 miners and surface workers were on short-term working.

In 1924 the Company reduced the workforce by 100 men, and closed the unprofitable seams.

The "Register for Mines" for 1926, recording the figures for the previous year, revealed that, with 111 men employed underground and 37 on the surface, it had been cut again in 1925.

"The Colliery Year Book and Trades Directory" for 1926 recorded the output for 1925, the last full year that the Pit worked, as 60,000 tons.

In May 1926 the local mineworkers joined the national miners' strike for higher wages. The strike crumbled after six months and the miners were forced to accept lower pay and longer hours.

When the Little Neston men returned to work they found the workings flooded, and the plant and machinery in need of a major overhaul. It was the best part of a month before they could start winning coal again.

The workforce was reduced again, to about sixty, in yet another attempt to keep the Pit open.

The discovery of a new, good-quality, seam that ran westwards under farmer Tommy Tozer's fields raised hopes that it could be saved, but negotiations over rights to work the seam broke down over terms.

All attempts to make the enterprise pay having failed, the Company finally submitted to liquidation.

The last shift was worked on 12th March 1927.

Asked whether he thought the new seam really would have saved the Pit, former miner George Tilley was emphatic. "Yes, I do. I saw the beginning of it. It was top-quality household coal. It shone so you could see your face in it. And it was six-feet thick - a piece of cake to work. It wouldn't have cost much to get it out and it could have been sold it at a good profit."

The Colliery was the biggest employer of labour in the Area, and its closure caused a serious local employment problem. Although some men moved out of the Area to find employment in other mines, unemployment remained a serious problem until the outbreak of the Second World War created as demand for manpower in the services and in war work.

SOURCES NOT MENTIONED IN THE TEXT

Birkenhead and Cheshire Advertiser and Wallasey Guardian, various issues.

Chambers, S., Hilditch, E., Place, G., and others "Neston 1840-1940" (The Burton and South Wirral History Society 1996)

Chester Chronicle, various issues.

Dawson, Greg., "Wyrale, Wirral Topics" (Dawson Publishing 1996)

Gilroy Geoffrey "Report on Coal and Ironstone Mines, the property of the Right Honourable Lord Mostyn and situate at park gate (sic), Cheshire." (Law, Hufsey, and Hulbert, Lincoln's Inn. March 1859).

Glegg Account Book (Held in the University of Liverpool Sidney Jones Library, Special Collections)

Lee, Bob, the late. (former miner) Author's recorded conversation with.

North of England Institute of Mining and Mechanical Engineering, Records of. Various documents referring to the Stanley Mine. Originals (Refs. WAT/3/71 and WAT/35) located at the Northumberland County Record Office. Copies now held at Cheshire County Record Office)

Peters, Joe, the late (former miner) Author's conversation with.

Sumner, Jim, the late (former clerk at Mine) Author's conversation with.

Tilley, George, the late. (former miner) Author's recorded conversation with.

Tudor, Joe, the late. (former miner) Author's recorded conversation with.

Appendix C

Neston Female Friendly Society

On the first Thursday of every June, Neston echoes to the sound of festival as the ladies of the local Female Friendly Society walk in procession through the town, drawing sightseers in their hundreds from the surrounding district.

Theirs is an organisation with a claim to distinction. Although a long-standing local tradition that it was the first such female society has now been disproved, it was certainly one of the first.

Founded in 1814, when official assistance for the penniless involved either the stigma of parish relief or the humiliation and hardships of the workhouse, such societies enabled ordinary women to achieve a measure of dignity that had previously been denied them.

The idea of forming a female friendly society seems to have been that of the Vicar, Prebendary Thomas Ward. An enlightened man, with views well in advance of his time, Ward was careful to limit his participation to calling an inaugural meeting and helping to draft the new Society's rules, before leaving the women to conduct their own affairs.

The original rules, which now hang in the Council Chamber of Neston Town Hall, include a list of the, forty or so, founder members. Unfortunately, the document is so badly faded that many names are now illegible, but, thanks to some diligent research work in the Parish Records by local historian Susan Chambers, a little is known about some of those whose names can be deciphered.

Mrs Chambers discovered, for example, that two Honorary Stewardesses, Frances Mary Ward and Arabella Monk, were appointed at the inaugural meeting. Frances Ward, aged twenty-one, was one of the Vicar's daughters. Twenty-six- year-old Arabella Monk was one of eleven surviving children of William Monk, a Parkgate Customs Officer, and his wife Esther, also a founder member.

Other founder members included Ann Elizabeth Ward, aged 25, another
of the Vicar's daughters, two doctors' wives, Mary Bond and Phoebe Cliffe,
teacher Maria Butler, and Margaret Sophia Wilson, who was to marry a
butcher in 1827.

Those present at that first meeting defined the objective of the proposed
Society as being,

> *For raising a fund by voluntary subscription, towards the support*
> *of the old, sick, lame, and infirm members thereof*

Interestingly, the rules have always stipulated that the Secretary shall be a
man. This was, almost certainly, because, in the early nineteenth century,
few women would have had the sort of business experience needed to fill
the post. Even so, the founders made sure that the appointment would not
expose them to the possibility of a male take-over. The same rule which
provided for the appointment of a male Secretary continues,

> *The Secretary shall, on all occasions, in the execution of his office,*
> *act under the superintendence, control, and direction of the*
> *Committee of Management.*

From the beginning, the Society's annual Anniversary Walk became an
occasion for a local holiday, when schools were closed, buildings were
draped with bunting, and all roads in Neston led to the High Street. Over
the years, it has become the day when all exiled Nestonians who can do so
return to their home town to renew old acquaintances and associations.

> *On the first of June,*

state the original rules,

> *....the members shall meet and walk in orderly procession to Church*
> *when an appropriate sermon shall be preached and, at four in the*
> *evening of the same day, the members shall meet again when they*
> *shall drink tea together.*

It then occurred to someone that, once every seven years, the first of June
would fall on the Sabbath, when such a celebration would be out of the
question. That being the case, the rules were changed to stipulate that the
Walk should be held on the first Thursday in June.

The founders did not, however, forget that the Society was all about
economy. To forstall the possibility of members impoverishing themselves
in some sort of unofficial internecine dress competition on the big day,
the rules also stipulated that they

> *.....shall not be otherwise dressed on that day than in stuff, printed*
> *linen, and cotton gowns on forfeiture of one shilling to the box.*

117

Known affectionately as "Ladies Club", the Society has for long been the subject of considerable local pride. Writing in praise of his adopted town towards the end of the last century, Neston poet James Stonehouse penned the following lines

A famous club
That female thrift imposes,
That marches through the town with flags,
A band and lovely posies.
There matrons mix with pretty girls,
With doctors and with clergy.
If these don't stir your heart's delight
There's nought on earth can urge ye.

As poetry they may leave something to be desired, but the pride is unmistakable.

For an institution that generates so much pride, the Society's affairs have remained remarkably free from controversy.

There was, it is true, just one unfortunate incident, in 1864. The Committee decided that the town band, the Band of the Neston Volunteers, was not playing well enough to lead the fiftieth Anniversary Walk, and invited the Band of the Chester Volunteers to do so.

It was a decision that rocked the town to its foundations, dividing the population into pro and anti Committee factions, and setting neighbour against neighbour.

The band members wasted little breath on argument. For them, the insult demanded action, not words. On the day of the Walk, they waited until the members of the Society were comfortably seated in the Church and the service had begun, and then formed up under the East Window, and launched into a cacophonous march. So loud was the noise that it brought the Vicar to a halt in mid-sentence, and prevented him from continuing. It was not until the Rector of Heswall, Mark Coxon, who was visiting Neston for the Walk, came out to remonstrate with the Band that they agreed to stop.

On the only other occasion that a similar situation arose the matter was resolved by negotiation and sweet reason. For 112 years the official celebrations had ended with country dancing to music provided by the brass band that played for the procession in the afternoon, but in 1926 a number of younger members asked the Committee to introduce modern dancing.

Bearing in mind the 1864 experience, the Committee asked the Secretary, Dick Wharham, to ascertain the attitude of the band to the proposed change before making a decision. To the surprise of many, the bandsmen were delighted with the proposal, which offered them the opportunity of enjoying the delights of the Charleston, the Black Bottom, and the Foxtrot, while others - the musicians of Woodhouse's Premier Orchestra - did the work.

While public interest has tended to centre on the Walk, the essential work of the Society - the task of mutual assistance - has continued quietly and efficiently every year since 1814. In return for their subscriptions, members claim sickness pay and maternity benefit whenever they are in need, and a payment is made towards funeral expenses when a member dies.

Until 1948, when the National Health Service was established, the Society operated its own health scheme, and the local doctors walked in the annual procession, robed in their academic gowns, as medical officers of the Society. After the government scheme had been implemented the Society discontinued its own scheme and the doctors withdrew from the walk.

One of the assurances the Society has always offered its members is that they will receive a decent and proper funeral. In the nineteenth century, and for much of the twentieth, when a pauper's funeral was a very real and humiliating prospect for many people, such an assurance was an important consideration.

Not only does the Society make a payment towards the cost of the funeral, it requires its members to honour their dead in their own traditional manner. As the coffin is carried from the hearse to the church they silently line both sides of the path, each member holding upright a plain white staff, at the top of which is tied a black crepe bow. As the coffin leaves the church, they again line the path in the same manner. It is a simple and yet strangely moving tribute. A monarch could not ask to be buried with greater dignity.

It is, however, the colourful Anniversary Walk that keeps the Society in the public eye and mind. Led by a band, the long procession of brightly-dressed women and girls makes its way down the High Street to the Parish Church. In their hands they carry the same white staves that they carry at funerals, but, instead of black crepe, they are garlanded with flowers and ribbons.

Before the procession, two stalwarts bear the Society's seven foot square banner, with its motif of clasped hands and text from St. Paul's letter to the Galatians,

"Bear Ye One Another's Burdens."

119

54. The officers and committee members of the Society photographed on Ladies' Day 1901. The man sitting on the ground is Edward Kerns, who was Secretary from 1893 until his death in 1908.

55. Ladies' Day 1901.

56. 1914. The Anniversary Walk passes the top of Brook Street.
(Collection Ian Boumphrey)

Over the course of the years, successive banners have deteriorated and been replaced, and there have been many variations in the design. A particularly interesting one was commissioned to mark Queen Victoria's Golden Jubilee. It bore a portrait of the Queen, with the dates 1837-1887, and the legend, "Long May She Reign in her People's Hearts." Economy being the watch-word of the Society, the banner remained in use well into Edward VII's reign.

Like many other ancient institutions, the Society has its mystery. Carried high towards the front of the procession is "The Dispensation", a staff that is surmounted by the Society's badge, and two large garlands. Both the origin of the Dispensation itself, and its name have been lost in the mists of time. Of the many theories that have been advanced, the most likely seems to be that the Society's original charter was once carried in a cylinder that was attached to the staff. But why "Dispensation"?

The Mayor, in his robes and chain of office, members of the local clergy, and many other local dignitaries walk, as the guests of the Society.

Inside the church the scene is as colourful as that in the High Street, with flowers packed on to every ledge that will hold them. Before taking their seats the members of the Society and the child walkers stand their staves in the umbrella holders at the end of the pews, transforming the aisles into avenues of flowers.

After the service the procession walks to the Cross, where a hymn and the National Anthem are sung. The walkers then disperse, to meet a little later for tea.

Sadly, changes have taken place over the years, and Ladies' Day is not the festival it once was. The advent of reasonably generous holidays for everyone has reduced the importance of the Event in the life of the community. Long gone are the pierrot shows that were a popular feature of the Day before the First World War. The dance, too, has gone, discontinued for lack of support, and, with it, the custom of adjourning to the town centre to dance around the Bushell monument until after midnight. Schools now remain open on Ladies' Day.

Within recent years, however, the Society has assumed an additional importance: it is now unique. All the other female friendly societies in the country have been disbanded, rendered obsolete by the welfare state. Only the ladies of Neston, conscious of their responsibility as the guardians of a tradition, walk in the footsteps of the pioneers of 1814.

SOURCES NOT MENTIONED IN THE TEXT

Councillor Norman Angel, former Secretary Neston F.F.S. Author's conversations with.

Birkenhead & Cheshire Advertiser & Wallasey Guardian, June 5th 1926

Birkenhead News, June 3 1939

Chambers, Susan, "Female Friendly Society" (Feature in Neston Civic Society Bulletin April 1989)

Chester Chronicle: Various issues

Original Rules of Neston Female Friendly Society. Framed copy in the Council Chamber of Neston Town Hall

Female Friendly Society File (Ref. 29F) at the Registry of Friendly Societies, 15 Great Marlborough Street, London.

Neston Female Friendly Society Rule Book, 1911

Stonehouse, James "Nestonian Lyrics" (1882) Copy in the Local History Collection, Neston Library

Appendix D

The Parkgate Ferries

The first regular ferry service across the Dee Estuary seems to have been established between Parkgate and Flint about 1740.

Before the introduction of the ferry, travellers who wished to cross the Estuary were obliged to use one of the hazardous so-called "sand roads", at low water.

The new service appears to have been well patronised because the demand for passage on the route soon exceeded the capacity of the available facilities. In 1786 a correspondent wrote to the Editor of "The Chester Chronicle" complaining that the service did not provide for the carriage of animals, and that travellers were obliged to leave their horses behind.

The deficiency was rectified three years later, when the following advertisement appeared in "Gore's Liverpool General Advertiser" dated November 5th 1789.

Parkgate and Flint Ferryboat

Thomas Spencer of the George Inn, Parkgate, and Daniel Jones of The Ship Inn, Flint, respectfully inform those ladies, gentlemen, and others travelling between the two places, that they have fitted up a large, commodious, Two Mast and Row Boat for the conveyance of Passengers, Horses, Cattle, etc., well manned with sober and experienced boatmen.

Passengers will be pleased to enquire for the boat called the "Llenwenney" at either of the above inns, or of Margaret Totty of Parkgate.

It was fortunate for the operators that there was, at the time, no such thing as a Trades Description Act, otherwise the reference to "sober and experienced boatmen" might have involved them in legal difficulties.

~ PARKGATE in 1791 ~

57 (a). Drawing of Parkgate, dated 22nd September 1791. Artist unknown. The building in the foreground, known at various times as "The Beer House", "The Ferry House", and, finally "The Pengwern Arms" was the Parkgate terminal for the Ferry service from at least 1814 to 1863. It was demolished about 1885, after having been extensively damaged by storms. (Collection Williamson Art Gallery)

57 (b). A recent photograph taken from approximately the same point where the artist stood to make the above drawing (Illustration 57a) "The Boathouse Restaurant" (built 1926) now occupies the site where the Pengwern Arms stood.

When two women were drowned in 1799 following the capsize of "The Friends" ferry boat, the editor of "The Chester Chronicle" commented:

The Flint and Parkgate boats have been used to carry too much sail in trying to out-sail each other, to the great danger and terror of the passengers.

Although the boatmen appear to have adopted a more responsible attitude by the time Richard Ayton made the crossing from Flint to Parkgate, in 1813, he still found the experience to be far from pleasant. Recording the journey in his book "A Voyage Round Great Britain", he wrote:

A packet boat sails regularly, when the tide permits from Flint to the opposite shore, and in this we took our passage, together with a crowd of other passengers, being packed and crammed into ones place with as little regard for our ease in such a state of stowage as though we had been dead cargo. It was proposed to us, as some comfort, that there was quite as much room on the present occasion as we should have found on any other day, and that nobody had ever made the passage with less reason to grumble. There are but two boats, and they can ply for only two hours of each flood. It is necessary, therefore, to load them at once, with as many as will consent to go together.

By that time the Parkgate landing place had moved to the Ferry House Inn, which stood on the site now occupied by the Boathouse Restaurant. (Illustrations 57a and 57b) Both the inn and the service was owned and operated by a certain J. Davies.

It was during Davies's tenure that an attempt was made to modernise the ferry. On 30th June 1817 "The Liverpool Mercury" published an announcement that a new steam packet, "The Ancient Briton," had begun sailing between Parkgate and Bagillt, making three round trips on each tide.

Travellers bound for Liverpool were carried by coach to Tranmere, to board a new Mersey steam boat, "The Regulator".

This co-ordinated service was brought to an early and sudden end in January 1818, when "The Regulator" sank in a gale. "The Ancient Briton" was sold to new owners on the Mersey, and, once more, the Dee crossings were made by sailing boats only.

No picture of "The Ancient Briton" appears to have survived, but a few details about her can be gleaned from an advertisement for the new service she provided, between Liverpool and Runcorn. Published in "Gore's

58. Thomas Johnson, Mine Host of the Pengwern Arms and stage coach/omnibus proprietor. Drowned on the last recorded trip of Parkgate ferry boat, 20th May 1864.

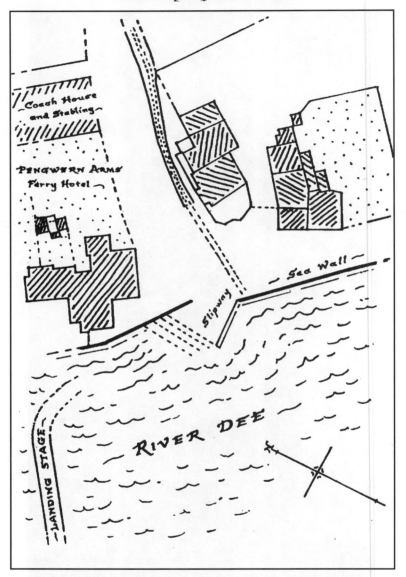

Map 8. The Pengwern Arms stood on the site now occupied by the Boathouse Restaurant.
(Adapted from the Mostyn Arms Estate Sale Map of 1849)

Liverpool Directory", it stated "The Ancient Briton's" engines were of 14 horse-power, and described the vessel as ....

> *The swiftest packet on the River Mersey, and her engine is so constructed that it cannot possibly be forced past its usual speed. The only communication with the safety valve is a chain instead of a rod of iron; therefore, no weight can be placed upon it as to prevent the overplus of steam escaping.*

The chain had been introduced, as a safety precaution, following a number of boiler explosions on the early steamships.

At the sale of the Mostyn Estate's Parkgate lands, in 1849, the Ferry House - by then known as "The Pengwern Arms" - and the ferry service passed into the hands of separate proprietors. The tenancy of the inn was acquired by Thomas Johnson, and the ferry service was bought by Joseph Railton, a former river pilot.

Even so, the two enterprises continued to offer a co-ordinated service. While Railton operated the ferry, Johnson provided both accommodation for those ferry passengers who needed it, and a coach service between Parkgate and Hooton Station on the newly-opened Chester to Birkenhead Railway line.

The regular ferry service came to an end with the death of Joseph Railton in June 1863.

What is probably the last recorded incident involving a Parkgate ferry boat was described in "The Chester Chronicle", of 28th May 1864, which reported the inquest on Thomas Johnson and his brother, Joseph, who had both been drowned on the 20th May, when trying to land from the boat in a heavy swell. It is possible that Johnson had been considering the revival of the ferry service because the fatalities occurred as he, Joseph, and others, were returning from a channel-surveying round trip to Bagillt.

Be that as it may, it is almost certain that any revived service would not have survived for long. The rapidly-developing , circuitous but more reliable, frequent, and comfortable, railway routes between Wirral and the towns of North Wales offered a far better way of travelling than the ferry.

SOURCES NOT MENTIONED IN THE TEXT

Neston Parish Registers

Place, G.W. "The Ferry Boat from Parkgate to Wales" (Paper)

Appendix E

The Cottage Hospital

When the temporary Red Cross Military Hospital, which had been housed in Neston Institute (now the Civic Hall), closed in 1919, the Treasurer reported a substantial cash balance in hand, together with a considerable amount of hospital equipment.

At the time there was a widely-expressed opinion that the Area needed a cottage hospital, and there was also a need to establish some form of suitable war memorial.

Both needs were met with the foundation of Neston and District War Memorial Cottage Hospital in 1920. A number of wealthy local people combined to buy "Dee View", a large sandstone house that stood on Little Neston Green, to accommodate the hospital, and a committee was formed to establish it. Initially, the hospital was staffed, furnished, and equipped to receive eleven patients, and the District Nurse, Christina Bell, was appointed Matron.

The new hospital was formally opened by the first Lord Leverhulme on 26th June 1920.

Until it was absorbed into the National Health Service, the hospital was completely independent. It was governed by an executive committee, which included representatives of various interested parties, like the local doctors, the hospital governors, Neston Urban District Council, and The Merseyside Hospitals Council, and financed entirely by fees, collections, donations, and investments.

Fees varied according to the accommodation and treatment provided, and according to whether the patient lived in the district or not. For example, a resident occupying a bed in one of the public wards paid 15 shillings a week, while a bed in a private ward cost £7.7.0. Patients from outside the district paid £1 for a bed in a public ward, or £8.8.0. for one in a private ward. And so on.

Many who could not afford to take such charges in their financial stride sought to insure against the day when they might need hospital treatment by joining one of the friendly societies then active in the area, such as the Oddfellows, the Shepherds, or Neston Female Friendly Society, which, together with other benefits, provided for hospital treatment. Others preferred "The Liverpool Penny in the Pound Scheme". Free accommodation and treatment was provided for the poorest of the poor.

Fees provided about two-thirds of the Hospital's annual income. The remainder came from voluntary contributions, and the investments made with some of the cash raised from those contributions.

From the beginning, the Cottage Hospital was the source of fierce local pride, and the focus of a remarkable sense of collective responsibility. Throughout its existence - even after it was absorbed into the National Health Service - contributions, both in cash and kind, flowed in from all parts of Neston Urban District.

Cash contributions came from donations made by individuals and various bodies, such as Neston Council and some of the district's social and sports clubs, and from legacies, church collections, collecting boxes placed in pubs and shops, and special events, like dances. The backbone of cash contributions was, however, the Subscriptions Scheme, a plan for covenanted giving. Subscribers were automatically registered as hospital governors, and, as such, they elected representatives on to the Executive Committee.

Gifts in kind included such items as books and periodicals, crockery and cutlery, flowers, fruit, and vegetables, and regular loads of farmyard manure.

The manure was used in the Hospital garden. Cultivated for most of its existence by staff gardener Sam Higgins, and, for the last few years, by his successor, Billy Lawton, the half-acre garden was generally acknowledged to be a great asset to the Hospital. Year after year, it yielded a steady supply of fresh fruit and vegetables for use in the wards, a capacity that was particularly appreciated during the Second World War.

The Hospital provided all the services expected of a general hospital at the time.

For the most part, patients were visited and treated by their own doctors.

The local doctors also carried out routine operations, like those for the removal of tonsils and appendices. There was, however, one serious problem involved in surgery. Although the hospital was furnished with a fine operating theatre, located on the ground floor (See illustration 62), it was not fitted with a lift. That being so, members of staff were obliged to man-handle patients from the private and semi-private wards, on the first floor, up and down the stairs, a task that involved six people. There being no porters on the staff, it was done by the theatre nurses and doctors. For long it was said that a lift could not be fitted because the building would not withstand the extra strain, but a lift was eventually installed, after the Hospital was incorporated into the National Health Service.

Consultants visited the Hospital regularly, and patients needing major surgery were transferred to Clatterbridge.

Open twenty-four hours a day, seven days a week, the Outpatients' Department dealt with a wide range of injuries, ranging from playground cuts and bruises to more serious injuries incurred on the roads, on the farms, and, in the early years, at the Mine.

An extension built in 1928 allowed the number of beds to be increased from nineteen to thirty-one. Later extensions housed the Physiotherapy Department and enlarged the Outpatients' Department.

Matron Bell retired on the 30th September 1934.

She was succeeded by Mildred Vickary, who resigned her post as a Sister at Victoria Central Hospital, Wallasey, to move to Neston.

The early years of the Second World War brought extra work for the Cottage Hospital in the shape of many patients evacuated from bomb-threatened hospitals at Birkenhead and Wallasey.

The Hospital was absorbed into the National Health Service on 1st January 1948.

In the late 1950s the operating theatre was closed, and all surgical cases were directed to Clatterbridge and the Hospital was downgraded to the status of a nursing home.

The Hospital was finally closed in 1964, and the building was demolished in 1967.

No doubt there were overwhelmingly good reasons why Neston War Memorial Cottage Hospital - like so many small hospitals throughout the country - should have been closed. No doubt that by concentrating human and other resources at large hospitals a far greater efficiency was achieved than under the old order. But, in achieving that efficiency, something valuable was lost. That something was the comfort which was brought to patients by the knowledge that they were being nursed in their own

59. The Cottage Hospital c. 1950. Note little Neston Methodist Church in the background, photographed here before the new porch was built.

Neston and District War Memorial Cottage Hospital.

Hon. Secretary
J. SMITH.
TELEPHONE 26 NESTON.

DEESIDE COTTAGE.
NESTON.
WIRRAL.

August 13th. 1934.

Miss. M. Vickary,
Victoria Central Hospital,
WALLASEY,
Cheshire.

Dear Madam,

I beg to inform you that at a Meeting of my Committee, held on Thursday evening, it was decided to accept your application for the position of Matron on the following conditions:-

1. That you commence duties as and from 1st. October.

2. SALARY - £100 per annum, payable quarterly, and £5 allowance for Uniform.

3. Four weeks holiday per annum to be allowed, also half a day per week and one whole day per month, the period of leave to be mutually agreed upon between yourself and the House Committee.

4. You to attend all operations, including any emergency cases that may happen in the night.

5. Three (3) months notice to be given on either side to terminate the engagement.

I shall be glad to hear if you agree to these conditions at your earliest convenience.

Yours faithfully,

J. Smith

HONORARY SECRETARY.

60. Letter offering Mildred Vickary the post of Matron.

134

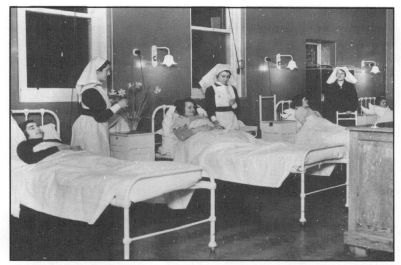

*61. The Women's Ward 1936. Matron Vickary (wearing cape)
checks that all is well.*

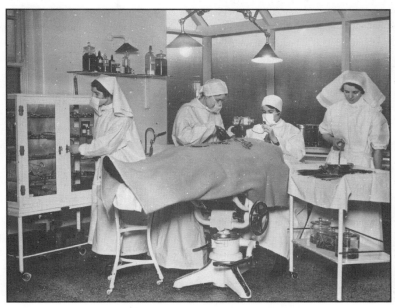

62. 1936. The Operating Theatre.

63. (opposite) Staff photograph taken on the eve of the hospital's closure.

From the left:

Back row: Mair Davis; Elsie Jones; Gladys Stallard; Agnes Hutchin; Sadie O'Byrne; ? Gilbertson; Clara Cottrell; Nancy Boswell; Mary Jellicoe; Edith Cottrell; Fanny Parry.

Front row: Dorothy Phillips; Bertha Kelsey; Mildred Vickary; Flora McIlroy; Olwen Whiteway; Enid Egner.

(Collection Elsie Jones)

community. They could look out of the windows and see their neighbours going about their everyday routines and, of course, it was very easy for relations and friends to visit them.

And, as a footnote, it should be recorded that the demolition of the handsome local sandstone building, with its prominent, spirit-lifting, spire, delivered a hard blow to the character and ambience of Little Neston Green.

SOURCES NOT MENTIONED IN THE TEXT

Author's interviews with former hospital Sisters Bertha Kelsey, Flora McIlroy, and Olwen Whiteway, former Junior General Duties Assistant Muriel Jones (later Sister at Clatterbridge Hospital), and former Cook-seamstress Elsie Jones.

Correspondence re. the appointment of Mildred Vickary as Matron. (Letters in private hands)

Author's own memories.

Neston and District War Memorial Cottage Hospital Annual Reports for 1943, 1944, 1945 (Silver Jubilee Year), and 1947-48.

Whiteway, Olwen "My Happy Memories of Old Neston" (Unpublished paper, 1993)